Letters Home

OF GOLD FIELDS, LOST SHIPS, AND SUNKEN TREASURE

CORRESPONDENCE FROM
THOMAS W. BADGER AND THOMAS N. BADGER
TO RELATIVES ON VIRGINIA'S EASTERN SHORE, 1863 – 1953

Compiled by
Curtis J., Lynn M., and Thomas H. Badger

SECOND EDITION

ISBN 978-1-62806-473-5   (print | paperback)

Published by Salt Water Media
29 Broad Street, Suite 104
Berlin, Maryland 21811
www.saltwatermedia.com

SALT WATER
MEDIA

Cover photo: Thomas Wyatt Badger, left, and John Wesley Badger in a daguerreotype probably taken in Baltimore, MD circa 1855.

Back cover photo: The *Central America* was built in 1852 and was originally named the *George Law*. This painting was done shortly after the ship was launched. Courtesy of the Mariners' Museum / Newport News, Va.

The first edition was previously published by Salt Water Media under ISBN 978-1-62806-060-7 with Library of Congress Control Number 2014956007

DEDICATION

This volume is dedicated to the extended family of Thomas W. Badger and Thomas N. Badger, which would include the Badgers, Tankards, Bells, Duntons, and Martins, among others. It also is dedicated to the memory of Susie Badger Kilham, whose interest in family history inspired the Badger-Tankard genealogy, published in 1973.

CONTENTS

INTRODUCTION TO THE SECOND EDITION

Since *Letters Home* was first published in 2014, more letters have been found, and more information has come forward. A packet of about 50 letters was in the estate of Margaret Badger Dunton and they became part of the larger collection, which is being donated to the Eastern Shore of Virginia Heritage Center. We are grateful to Ned and Joan Duer McMath for the gift. Joan is the great-granddaughter of Margaret Badger Dunton, whose father was John Wesley Badger of Red Bank.

The new letters shed light on the early years of Thomas N. Badger and the final years of his uncle Capt. Thomas W. Badger. The collection now documents the lives in full of both these men. The new additions document Thomas N.'s teenage years as a student at VMI, and they capture the painful final days of Thomas W. in letters written from Thomas N. to his father back home in Red Bank.

The wonderful thing about these letters is that they bring history to life. They not only document events, but over time they allow the personalities and temperaments of people to develop. In reading them, I often was amazed at how someone who lived one hundred years ago reminds me of a cousin I know well today. And at times I see myself in my ancestors. Like Thomas N., I was not a gifted student in school, nor did I enjoy working for others to earn a salary. He found his footing when he discovered what he wanted to do and then set out to do it on his own. Our family has had many men who were farmers, and few who held what might be termed a regular job. I don't farm, but it has been years since I had a regular job. Thank you for paving the way, Uncle Tom.

This new edition also introduces a third-generation Thomas Badger who has made the transcontinental migration. Tom, the son of Curtis and Lynn and grandson of Thomas Hallett Badger, has settled in Oregon, but he has spent time re-tracing the roots of his ancestors in the San Francisco and Oakland area. In the final chapter Tom locates the home where Thomas N. lived, and he discovers the surprising resting place of Thomas W. and many of his fellow California Pioneers.

THE BADGER LETTERS

On March 3, 1849 Thomas Wyatt Badger, age 22, and his younger brother, John Wesley Badger, 17, left the family farm at Red Bank Landing in Northampton County, Virginia and set out for the California gold fields. This began a relationship with the Badger family and the state of California that would last for more than a century. Although John moved back to Virginia prior to the Civil War, Thomas lived most of his life in the San Francisco and Oakland area. He was a ship owner, the owner of an amusement park, a marine surveyor, and an adventurer and entrepreneur.

Thomas's nephew, Thomas Norman Badger, was born on the family farm at Red Bank on December 2, 1867. He enrolled in the Virginia Military Institute in Lexington when he was 16, attended for about two years studying civil engineering, and returned home to teach school. He subsequently left for Washington, D.C. and Philadelphia to work as a civil engineer before deciding to follow his uncle's example and seek his fortune in California. He moved to Berkeley in 1890 and set up a business as a surveyor and town planner, designing residential communities such as Emeryville in the Berkeley area. One

Thomas Norman Badger

1

Thomas Wyatt Badger, left, and John Wesley Badger in a daguerreotype probably taken in Baltimre, MD circa 1855

of his first jobs upon arriving in California was to draw a map of his uncle's park.

Both Badgers were prolific letter writers, and the 100-or-so letters that have survived add a third dimension to family genealogy. We read the letters and go beyond the lines and graphs of family who-begat-whom. We get a glimpse of their personalities, their relationships, their

Five Generations of the Badger Family

From Coast to Coast

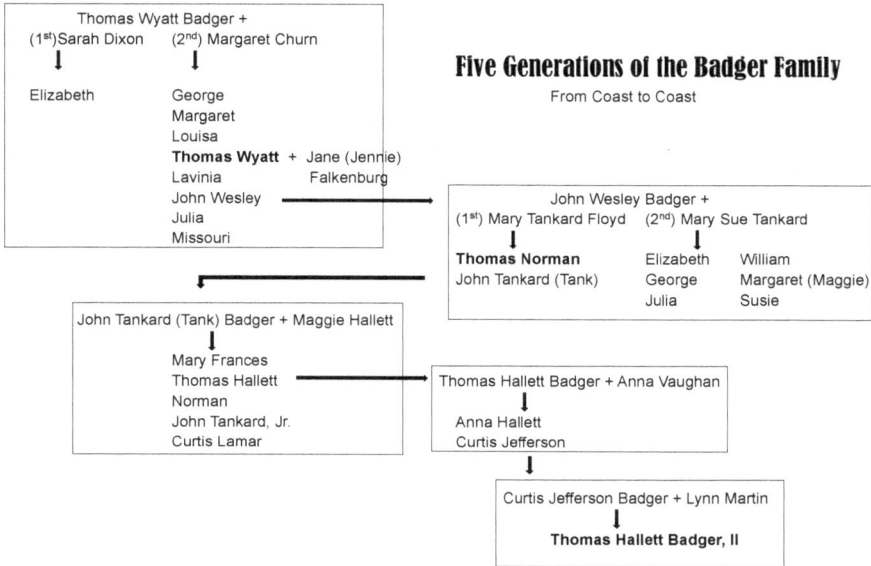

Thomas Wyatt Badger +
(1st) Sarah Dixon   (2nd) Margaret Churn

Elizabeth   George
             Margaret
             Louisa
             Thomas Wyatt + Jane (Jennie)
             Lavinia   Falkenburg
             John Wesley
             Julia
             Missouri

John Wesley Badger +
(1st) Mary Tankard Floyd   (2nd) Mary Sue Tankard

Thomas Norman   Elizabeth   William
John Tankard (Tank)   George   Margaret (Maggie)
                         Julia   Susie

John Tankard (Tank) Badger + Maggie Hallett

Mary Frances
Thomas Hallett
Norman
John Tankard, Jr.
Curtis Lamar

Thomas Hallett Badger + Anna Vaughan

Anna Hallett
Curtis Jefferson

Curtis Jefferson Badger + Lynn Martin

Thomas Hallett Badger, II

hopes, and their despair. We read about events dealing with the Civil War and Reconstruction, about local news such as a duel in Eastville, and tragedies such as the sinking of a ship in the South China Sea that took the life of young George T. Martin of Hacks Neck, the son of Louisa Badger Martin and Smith Kendall Martin.

Most of the letters are written to fathers and brothers. Thomas Wyatt wrote often to John Wesley, his brother, who was back on the family farm at Red Bank. The letters begin during the Civil War, in 1863, and they end in 1953, when Thomas N. was nearing the end of his life. Thomas N. wrote many letters to his father, John, and later to his younger brother, John Tankard Badger, whom everyone knew as Tank. The letters to his father are affectionate, enthusiastic, and deferential. The letters to his brother reveal a darker side of his life, worries about money and health, a desperation that becomes more and more urgent as the years pass.

There also are a few letters written by and to various other friends and family members, but the main narrative thread is the relationship between the two sets of brothers, the young pair who sought their fortunes in gold, and the next generation of John Tankard and Tom who carried on a transcontinental correspondence by mail for four decades.

We're fortunate that these letters survive. Our family's parents, grandparents, and great-grandparents did a wonderful job of safekeeping them. There are gaps, of course, and we have to sometimes read between the lines to fill in the narrative. And, unfortunately, there are no letters from John to Tom, and so we are privy to only one side of the dialog. It is somewhat sad to realize that ours will likely be the last generation to examine the day-to-day lives of our ancestors through the written word. E-mail messages are rarely stored away in attics for generations as these letters were.

We have tried to add context to the letters by coupling them with news events, family events, and genealogical notes, taken mainly from the book *The Badger and Tankard Families of the Eastern Shore of Virginia* compiled by Austin D. Killham in 1973. The book was begun by Austin's wife, Susie, the youngest daughter of John W. Badger and Mary Sue Tankard Badger. She died before completing the manuscript. Information on land transfers came from Ralph T. Whitelaw's *Virginia's Eastern Shore – A History of Northampton and Accomack Counties.* Information on the sinking of the ship *Central America* came from *The Final Voyage of the Central America 1857* by Normand E. Klare, who also had ancestors aboard the ship. Much information on the early days of California was provided by the Society of California Pioneers. The painting of Thomas W. Badger's home was provided by the Oakland Museum of California, and other information on his life in California was taken from the museum website.

John Tankard "Tank" Badger

The Home Place

The Badger family became established in the colonies in the early 17th century. Records list a John Badger living in Jamestown in 1622, and Edmund and Elizabeth Scarborough sold 150 acres to Reynold (or Reginald) Badger in 1693. This land, according to Ralph T. Whitelaw's *Virginia's Eastern Shore*, was between what is now Onley and Melfa on the east side of U.S. Rt. 13. Nathaniel Badger is buried here, on a tract known as the Phillips Farm.

But the Badgers were predominantly a Northampton County family, becoming established on the seaside on Red Bank Creek near Marionville in the late 1700s. Thomas Wyatt Badger was born in Accomack County on the Fourth of July 1786, one decade after the signing of the Declaration of Independence. He was the son of Nathaniel Badger, and his mother was Joyce Wyatt Edmunds Badger, the widow of Thomas Edmunds.

He had an older brother, also named Nathaniel, who was eleven years his senior and apparently something of a father figure. Thomas's father stipulated in his will that his 125-acre farm and home would go to the elder son, Nathaniel Jr., with the condition that Nathaniel "shall provide education for Thomas in reading, writing, and ciphering until Thomas reaches 15 years of age." If he failed to do so, the 125-acre farm would be split between the two. There is no record of Thomas owning the land, so he must have learned to read, write, and cipher sufficiently.

Thomas appears to have been a bright, ambitious, and responsible young man. He had four step-brothers whose father was Thomas Edmunds, but he, the youngest of the six, was clearly the favorite son. His mother died in 1810 and in her will left "one shilling and nothing

John Wesley Badger in 1901

more" to the four Edmunds men and to Nathaniel, Jr. The remainder of her estate went to Thomas Wyatt Badger. This will was recorded in Northampton County, so it is probable she moved to Northampton with Thomas Wyatt after the death of her husband in 1795.

Thomas Wyatt was living in Northampton in the early 1800s when he fell in love with Sally Dixon, whose family was from the Thomas's Wharf area on the seaside near Marionville. Sally was the daughter of Thomas and Bridget Dixon who lived on a 100-acre farm known as Marionville Plantation. Thomas Dixon died in 1798, Bridget died in 1806, and as the only child Sally inherited Marionville Plantation from her mother. In her will written on May 7, 1805, Bridget stated "I lend to my daughter Sally Dixon my whole estate and my wearing apparel until such time as she has a lawful heir, then I give the said property to her and her heirs forever. But if in case that she should not have a lawful heir, I give said estate to my nieces, Polly Thomas and Betsey Thomas, the daughters of Harrison Thomas and Betsey his wife to be equally divided between them." The will was probated on December 8, 1806.

Red Bank Baptist Church in Marionville, founded in 1783, was the spiritual center of the seaside community. Folks gathered to worship on the Sabbath, the departed were interred in the neighboring cemetery, and young couples were united in the small chapel. On October 10, 1808 Thomas Badger and Sally Dixon were wed at Red Bank Baptist Church by the Rev. Isaac Bratton, and they began a life together farming Marionville Plantation.

In 1811 the young couple added on to their acreage. Perhaps using the inheritance received from his mother the previous year, Thomas bought a 111-acre farm called Cedar Plain, today known as the Dunton farm. According to deed books in the Northampton County clerk's office, Thomas bought the land from John and Hannah Waddey for the sum of 388 pounds, 10 shillings. Cedar Plain became the home place for numerous generations of the Badger and Dunton families. Many of them are buried in the family cemetery on the farm.

At the tender age of 25, Thomas had a growing farm operation, and life must have been good for the young couple. They owned fertile land, they enjoyed fishing and gathering shellfish in the nearby waters of Red Bank Creek and Hog Island Bay, and very soon their family would grow. Elizabeth P. Badger was welcomed to the world on November 6, 1812, and the land that had been "lended" to Sally now legally belonged to her and her heirs.

The young Badger family must have been living a life of promise and prosperity in the fall of 1812, but events happening far away, on a world stage, would soon shatter the tranquility of their rural home. In the early 1800s the British and French were involved in an on-going conflict known as the Napoleonic Wars. The United States declared its neutrality and tried to trade freely with the belligerent parties, and this angered both the British and the French, who attempted by various means to interfere with U.S. trade and the rights of American citizens.

On June 18, 1812, at the request of President James Madison, the United States declared war on Britain. To the young family, this must have seemed a distant and somewhat amorphous event. Trouble on the trade routes? What sort of threat could that pose to life on a remote seaside farm on the rural Eastern Shore? But within a year, Thomas Badger – farmer, husband, and father – would be wearing a uniform and carrying a musket. The life of the young family would never be the same.

The War of 1812 came to the rural Eastern Shore as the British attacked American merchant ships in the Chesapeake Bay. The British established fortifications on Tangier Island and used Tangier as a base for the duration of the war. From there they sent ships to attack Washington and Baltimore and smaller towns such as Havre de Grace, which was burned. While Eastern Shore communities were not necessarily military targets, the British sent raiding parties ashore looking for food, livestock, and anything else of value. The British also recruited slaves, promising them freedom in exchange for fighting on their side.

The task of protecting local people fell to the militia, a group of brave, but poorly armed and poorly trained citizen soldiers. Thomas joined the 27th Regiment of the Militia of Virginia in Northampton County. He was a corporal in Captain Matthew H. Dunton's company, and the regiment was commanded by Lt. Col. Major S. Pitts. Most of the men in the militia were farmers and merchants, Pitts was a county official, and none of them were well equipped, trained, or accustomed to firing a deadly weapon at a fellow human being. Members of the militia served on an as-needed basis for the most part. Thomas served from September 8 to 18 in 1813, and from August 29 to September 29 in 1814. The militia members were also mustered when word went out that a British attack was imminent.

The family of John W. Badger gathered for Thanksgiving dinner at the farm at Red Bank Landing in November 1901. Seated are, from left, Susie Badger, Margaret Badger, Aunt Easter Badger (see Appendix D). Standing are, from left, Edward Anderson, Bessie Badger Anderson, William Badger, John Wesley Badger, Sue Tankard Badger, George Henry Badger, and Lavinia Badger LeCato Kelley. The patriarch of the famiy died on August 1, 1905.

According to the Badger-Tankard genealogy, Thomas was taken prisoner by the British, held in a fort in Canada, and his wife Sally died while he was imprisoned. This intriguing but sketchy detail from the genealogy is difficult to substantiate. The dates Thomas served in the Virginia militia were confirmed in the Library of Virginia, but the National Archives in Washington, D.C. has no records of Thomas serving in the military or of being held prisoner by the British.

But considering the broader aspects of what was happening in the War of 1812 at that time, it is very possible that he was indeed taken prisoner, although "kidnapped" might be a more apt term. Prisoners were regularly taken by both sides and were usually held for a time and then swapped for fellow prisoners – wartime bargaining chips as it were.

The American navy included a large number of privateers, privately-owned fighting ships licensed to plunder enemy ships in exchange for cargo, which could be sold at a nice profit. According to Alan Taylor's

The Civil War of 1812, in March 1814 the Americans encouraged the privateers to take prisoners by offering a $100 bounty per head. This enraged the British, who "raided the coast of the Chesapeake Bay to grab citizens, whether acting in the militia or not, and sent them to the prison at Halifax, Nova Scotia." This could be what happened to Thomas. The British had a naval prison on Melville Island in Halifax.

Although the records of the Virginia militia indicate that Thomas spent a month in service during the summer of 1814, he could have been away for much longer than that. The War of 1812 effectively ended on Christmas Eve 1814 in the Flemish city of Ghent, when British and American officials signed a treaty restoring relations between the two countries. The treaty was ratified by the British Parliament and American Senate a few weeks later. It is possible that Thomas could have been held until the end of the war in late 1814 or early 1815. It is not known when Sally died, or what the cause might have been. There is no marker with her name in the Badger cemetery at Cedar Plain.

With the war over, Thomas Badger was free to resume his life on the farm, although it must have been a bittersweet return. He was no doubt thrilled to be reunited with 2-year-old Elizabeth, but Sally's death while he was in prison no doubt left a void that would not soon be filled.

Another chapter of his life began on December 28, 1818 when 32-year-old Thomas took as his bride 23-year-old Margaret Churn, the daughter of Severn Churn and Tamor Meholloms Churn. Margaret would become the step-mother of 6-year-old Elizabeth, and she and Thomas would have eight more children of their own. Among them would be Thomas Wyatt and John Wesley, who would one day seek their fortune in the California Gold Rush.

Elizabeth grew up, and in 1833 married George Bell, Jr. Four years later Thomas would give them the farm that had been Sally's parents' property, honoring the wish of Bridget Dixon that the land go to Sally's heirs. Elizabeth and George lived there their entire lives, raising eight children. According to the Badger-Tankard genealogy, two of them became doctors, and another a Presbyterian minister.

Thomas bought more property in the area on May 2, 1842 when he purchased 105 acres on Red Bank Creek from Smith and Margaret

Bell for $1,305.50. Red Bank Landing would later become the property of Thomas Wyatt Badger, but it would be the home of John Wesley, who would build a large residence there when his Gold Rush adventures ended. It says in Badger-Tankard that John inherited the Cedar Plains property and Thomas was given the Red Bank place. John turned the Cedar Plains property over to his sister Margaret, who wanted to live out her days in the old home place, and he moved to the Red Bank farm, which Tom allowed him to use rent-free as he saw fit. Later in life, realizing he would never return to Virginia, Tom relinquished his ownership to John.

After buying the Red Bank place, Thomas lived only four more years. He died on October 18, 1846 at age 60. His wife, Margaret, died on June 24, 1855. Both are buried in the family cemetery at Cedar Plain.

Three years after the death of their father, Thomas and John Badger left for California to seek their fortunes in the Gold Rush. John returned to Virginia prior to the Civil War, but Thomas lived most of his adult life in the San Francisco area. He created a shipping company, with vessels trading all over the coast. He built a large home on ten acres on an inlet overlooking San Francisco Bay, and he added extensive gardens, outbuildings, and a large windmill to provide fresh water. In 1872 he retired from shipping and turned his 10-acre home into Badger's Grand Central Park, which included a dance hall, ten pin alley, pavilion, restaurant, gardens, museum, and a sailing pond.

In 1856 Thomas married Jane A. Falkenburg, the widow of his partner in the shipping business, Capt. Charles Falkenburg. Thomas was bringing his bride home to meet the family in September 1857 aboard the sidewheeler *Central America* when the ship foundered in a hurricane off the coast of South Carolina. The ship went down, taking the lives of some 400 passengers. Thomas and Jane survived the sinking and were reunited with the family on the Eastern Shore, but they longed to return to California.

By the time the Civil War broke out in 1861, they were back in California for good. Captain Tom was a Californian who had inherited from his father a 111-acre farm on the Eastern Shore seaside called Red Bank Landing. John, having passed along his inheritance, Cedar Plain, to his sister, lived on Tom's property with his permission to "live on it as if it were your own."

And that is exactly what John did. When I was a child the home there was derelict and had not been lived in for years, but I remember massive grape arbors, flooring of heart pine, and a potato cellar under a trap door in what must have been the kitchen. But my great aunt, Susie Badger Kilham, who grew up in the home, wrote a wonderful description of the property in the Badger-Tankard genealogy:

"John made a well-constructed addition to the kitchen step-up, dining room step-up. These step-ups were characteristic of the weatherboard houses of the time on the Eastern Shore. (They are all now fast rotting down.) The room above the downstairs bedroom had a sloped roof. John built a hall with stairway up to a hall and two bedrooms, a portico room and parlor chamber upstairs and a good sized parlor downstairs with five windows. His life in California influenced him. For instance, there was a door from the portico room to the porch roof with a pair of pivoted louvered blind doors. The same led from the downstairs hall to the flower garden at the side. A larger door led from the hall to the porch. The porch extended across the front of the main part of the house. There were two wide steps from porch to ground and they were of one board each. These improvements were of heart pine and good brick as evidenced today since it has not fallen down.

John built a garden with a large scuppernong grape arbor extending above and across the drive. Many guests usually drove past the back door rather than in the front from Red Bank Landing. This arbor covered the area at the back of the house and was shady and cool and easy of access from the dining room and kitchen. Here we lived a great deal of the time. Large grape arbors indicated the Spanish influence.

The grape arbor, with many varieties of grapes, then extended over the main axis of the garden – the central path and the intersecting lateral path. At the end of the main axis the path turned at right angles and went on for about two miles (my legs were short) to the Garden House. At the ends of the lateral path and the axis path were fig bushes. The garden was primarily a fruit garden with cherries, peaches, figs, grapes, apples, pears (including the Duchess, which is unavailable now), plums, walnuts, plus

The home place at Red Bank Landing had a large garden and grape arbor. This photograph was taken circa 1900.

several hives of bees. There were also some flowers – lilac, sweet shrub, moss rose, roses, English bluebells, and others. In the front yard was a tremendous mulberry tree, very tall, three or four feet in diameter, and about 13 feet in circumference."

All of this today is gone, reclaimed by woodland and salt marsh. The family moved to a mainland farm in Birds Nest in 1905, reflecting the great change brought to the Eastern Shore in 1884 with the opening of the railroad. My great-grandfather was a farmer and seaman, and Red Bank Landing was both his farm and his home port. With the coming of the railroad, commerce gradually moved from the boat landings to the railroad stations. My family continued to farm the land for years, but the fields were small, and the low areas were slowly reverting to salt marsh. My uncle Lamar was the last to plow the land. In 1986, the farm was sold to The Nature Conservancy with a conservation easement limiting development. Today it is all pine woods and salt marsh.

OFF TO CALIFORNIA

Like many young men in America in 1849, Thomas and John Badger dreamed of striking it rich in the gold fields of California. Their father had died in 1846 when Thomas was 19, and he had become the leader of the family. At 15 he had taken a job as a mate on a cargo vessel, and thus began his life as a seaman.

In 1848 word spread around the world that James Marshall had discovered gold near Sutter's Fort in California. Suddenly, men by the tens of thousands took off to seek fortune and adventure in the gold fields of the west. Some traveled across country, and others came by boat. Thomas and John were both experienced sailors, so they chose the latter method of travel. They left their home port of Red Bank and sailed north to New York, and on March 3, 1849 they boarded the schooner *James L. Day* for California. It was a long and arduous journey, during which John became ill with what probably was yellow fever. In a letter years later, his son, Thomas N. Badger, mentioned that his father had once suffered from "jungle fever," and continued to be bothered by "nerve problems." It took them nearly six months to reach California.

The brothers sailed from New York around Cape Horn, and then took a northern route up the coast. It was a long trip, made even longer by currents and prevailing winds that forced ships to make a wide swing nearly to the longitude of the Hawaiian Islands. This would be the last journey of this distance they would have to endure. One of the many issues raised by the California Gold Rush was the need to efficiently get men and materials to the mining areas in California, and to get gold back to banks and mints in the east. A railroad across the swampy isthmus of

Panama shortened the journey by thousands of miles and saved weeks of travel time.

The railroad opened in 1855, eliminating the voyage around Cape Horn. The tracks stretched across 47 miles of swamp and jungle, linking western Panama City with Aspinwall, a railroad town built on the eastern terminus and named for William H. Aspinwall, the president of the rail company. In 1890 the name was permanently changed to Colon, honoring the explorer Christopher Columbus.

The journey on the single-track railroad took about six hours, and descriptions of the trip vary from "a rickety affair" to "uneventful and all too short." Never-the-less, it greatly shortened the journey of sailing from coast to coast.

Thomas and John arrived in San Francisco in August 1849, and, unfortunately, there are no records to document their adventures during the first months and years of the Gold Rush. Did they discover gold? Perhaps. Evidence seems to indicate that the brothers thrived in California, especially Thomas. Thomas went into the shipping business with Capt. Charles Falkenburg, who appeared to be just as much of an adventurer as he was. The two men owned several ships, and they did business from Mexico to the South China Sea. Did gold finance their shipping business? Or did they simply profit from having a shipping business when commerce was at its peak?

They clearly were successful businessmen. Capt. Falkenburg was an expert sailor who set a speed record making the crossing to Manilla. He had sailed from Boston to San Francisco via Cape Horn aboard the barquentine *Jane A. Falkenburg*, arriving on New Year's Day 1855. With him was his wife and the namesake of his ship, Jane A. Falkenburg. Capt. Falkenburg enjoyed the thrill of speed on both land and sea. He and Jane were planning a trip to Sydney, Australia, but before they could leave, Capt. Falkenburg was killed while racing his carriage down Telegraph Hill. In a matter of months, his widow and his business partner would become husband and wife.

Evidence provided by letters written years after the Gold Rush suggests that Thomas, who had been at sea since age 15, prospered in the shipping business, and John spent time in the gold fields. Thomas wrote

John several times and made reference to the period when John lived in Weaverville. Weaverville is in northern California in Trinity County and is one of the original Gold Rush settlements. It was home to some 2,000 Chinese prospectors who came looking for gold. If John was living in Weaverville, chances are he was active in the gold fields. Newspaper account from the day suggest that John might have worked in the gold fields for a period of time, and later became involved in the mercantile business, providing goods and services for those who were prospecting.

An account in the May 15, 1858 edition of the *Trinity Journal* of Weaverville states that "John W. Badger's cabin was burned on East Weaver, last Friday, with all his provisions." On April 16, 1859 the same newspaper reported that John W. Badger was working on a project to bring water to the community. "Mr. John Badger intends to bring clear water from East Weaver creek to an elevated reservoir in Faggtown, whence it may be conveyed in pipes to all the residents there...A stream clear and pure and five inches square, will be supplied – enough for all purposes, including irrigation."

So, after John lost his cabin and provisions, he apparently decided that it was more prudent to go into business rather than compete with others in the search for gold. A letter from Wiley Tinnin to John Badger in Red Bank in July 1891 indicates that the two had been in the mercantile business in Weaverville.

John left Weaverville in the summer of 1860 to return home. The prospects of civil war probably influenced his decision to return to the home farm at Red Bank. The *Trinity Journal* published this item in the July 7, 1860 edition:

> *Ira Howe, John W. Badger, and Bennet Cook, all old citizens, sail on the next steamer for the States. The first goes to Bombay, N.Y., the second to Pungoteague, Va., and the last to Fall River, Mass. We know their destination because each subscribed for the Journal before leaving.*

So John's tenure as a Californian lasted eleven years. He and his brother Tom arrived in August 1849 and by August 1860 he was back at Red Bank. John farmed the land and was in the shipping business and

The town of Weaverville began as a Gold Rush town in Northern California and today is the seat of Trinity County. John Badger lived there for about ten years, returning to Virginia months before the Civil War broke out.

was active in running the Union blockade early in the war. John shipped goods from Red Bank Landing all over the east coast and south to the West Indies. According to the Badger-Tankard book, John registered his schooner *Louisiana* in Vienna, Maryland so he could get through the federal lines during the Civil War. He ran the Union blockades for quite a while until he was caught off the coast of North Carolina on his way home from Puerto Rico. His schooner was seized and he was briefly jailed. After the war he bought another schooner named the *Panama* and used it to ship produce along the east coast.

So, the brothers seemed to have prospered during their time in California. Did they find gold, or were they simply good businessmen who were lucky to be in the right place at the right time? No one in the family has a gold piece they might have found, so perhaps they found none. On the other hand, they could have discovered gold in California, and today it could be resting on the bottom of the sea.

The Sinking of the *Central America*

When visiting family back home in Virginia, Thomas would take a ship from Oakland to Panama, cross the isthmus by rail, and board another ship for the second leg of his journey. He knew the sea well and preferred traveling by ship to overland travel. He first went to sea at age 15, working as a deck hand on various boats sailing out of east coast ports. By the time he was in his twenties, he was the captain of his own ship.

Thomas liked to take the *Central America* from Panama to New York. He had sailed on the *Central America* three times prior to the fall of 1857, and he was very familiar with the ship. He once described her as "one of the best and staunchest ships afloat." Tom and Jane Falkenburg were married in late 1856, and in September 1857 they planned a honeymoon trip aboard the *Central America* to introduce her to the folks back home.

The *Central America* was by all accounts a handsome ship. She was a steam powered, three-masted sidewheeler, built in New York in 1852 and originally christened the *George Law*. She was now owned by the U.S. Mail Steamship Company, and her master was Capt. William Lewis Herndon, who, like Thomas, went to sea at age 15. Capt. Herndon, now 44, was a Navy veteran who had risen to the rank of commander in 1855. He had taken a leave of absence from the Navy to take the helm of the *Central America* two years earlier. This would be the ship's 45th voyage from Panama to New York.

Capt. Herndon and his crew had sailed from New York on August 22, 1857, heading for Panama. On the same day in San Francisco, Capt. Tom and Jennie, as he called her, boarded the *Sonora* and headed south. They would link up with the *Central America* in early September at

The **Central America** *was built in 1852 and was originally named the* **George Law.** *This painting was done shortly after the ship was launched. (Courtesy of the Mariners' Museum / Newport News, Va.)*

Aspinwall, and from there travel north to New York and visit family in Virginia.

The *Central America* arrived in Aspinwall on September 2, and the crew quickly began restocking the ship with coal, food for the passengers, medicine, rigging, and other supplies. One hundred bags of mail and several tons of gold were transferred from the *Sonora*. The United States Mint opened in San Francisco in 1854, and there were freshly minted gold coins, heavy gold bars, and money of private coinage. Consignees, including the American Exchange Bank and Wells Fargo and Company, had $1.6 million in gold secured in the *Central America's* hold. In addition, many passengers carried large sums of their own. Thomas and Jennie carried a valise with $20,000 in gold pieces.

The *Central America* was loaded, inspected, and ready to set sail. At 4:15 p.m. on September 3 Capt. Herndon gave the order to cast off. The ship, fully loaded with nearly 600 passengers and crew, was on its way north. The first stop would be Havana, Cuba.

It took exactly four days to reach Havana, and it had been beautiful cruising weather, blue skies with a nice breeze, warm days and cool nights. During the brief layover, some of the men went ashore to stock up on Cuban cigars, which were very popular in America and were being imported by the millions annually. It was hurricane season in the tropics, but all was calm in Havana. The current topic of concern was a yellow fever outbreak, not the weather.

The *Central America* left for New York shortly after breakfast on Tuesday, September 8, still sailing under clear skies and a brisk breeze. Passengers passed the time by strolling on the promenade deck or reading books, newspapers, and magazines. Card playing was popular among the men.

On Wednesday at 5:30 a.m., Second Officer Frazer noted in the ship's log that Cape Florida passed 75 nautical miles to the west. At noon he noted that there was a fresh breeze and head sea, and that since leaving Havana the *Central America* had traveled 286 nautical miles.

The weather quickly began to deteriorate on Wednesday afternoon. The barometer dropped, the rain began, and the wind began to blow with the force of a gale. Most of the passengers believed the storm would pass during the night, and they would awake to find clear skies in the morning. On Thursday, it was obvious that the *Central America* had sailed into a hurricane. Thomas arose at 6 a.m. and by 7:30 he and Jennie were on the deck. Thomas went below and noticed that the ship's engine appeared to labor sailing into the heavy seas, and that the chief engineer seemed concerned. He checked back later in the day and noticed that the engine was running even slower.

On Friday the storm continued unabated, as the *Central America* followed the track of the hurricane as it made its way northeast up the coast. Thomas noted on Friday morning that the ship was "free from water, with head to the wind, laying very easy, and engine working slowly." At 9 a.m. the chief engineer reported that the leeward bilge was taking on water. Captain Herndon ordered that the pumps be used, but they failed to reduce the water level. The ship's list, and the violence of the sea, made it impossible for the coal passers to use wheelbarrows, so Captain Herndon ordered all available crew to use buckets and baskets to pass coal to the engine room. It was essential to keep steam up and to keep the bow into the sea.

A second leak was discovered around a shaft leading from the engine to the starboard paddle, and at 11 a.m. Captain Herndon met with passengers in the first class cabin area and asked the men to form bucket brigades to pass coal and to bail water from the steerage area. By noon water had covered the floor in the coal storage bunker and the ship lost power. Seas broke over the decks and flooded the staterooms.

Through the day and into the night men bailed water, but to no avail. At daybreak the captain ordered the flag hoisted half-mast in a signal of distress. The *Central America* was in a frequently used shipping lane, and the hope now was to keep the ship afloat until the passengers could be rescued. The men bailed continuously for 22 hours before a sail appeared on the horizon at 1 p.m. on Saturday.

The brig *Marine* of Boston had taken on a load of molasses in Cardena, Cuba and was heading north when she passed to the lee of the stricken *Central America*. Capt. Herndon hailed the brig and asked the captain, Hiram Burt, to lay by, as the *Central America* was in "a sinking condition." Capt. Burt replied that he would remain as long as he could.

The *Marine*, which itself had been battered by the storm, stood by to take on passengers, and women and children would be the first to go. Although the worst of the storm had passed, there still were 30-foot seas, making the task of loading, unloading, and rowing the lifeboats extremely difficult. To further complicate things, the *Marine* was not capable of maneuvering close to the *Central America* and was slowly drifting away. Crews of both vessels worked steadily throughout the afternoon, and by evening all of the women and children had been transferred, as well as a few of the men.

As darkness fell, those remaining on the *Central America* realized that they would not be rescued by the *Marine*, and most realized that the ship would not make it through the night. The men put on what life preservers and metal life buoys they could find, and doors and other wooden structures were gathered to be used as rafts.

The *Central America* went under stern-first, and as she entered into the sea she took along hundreds of men, who were sucked into the void left by the ship. Some re-surfaced, but many did not survive the first ten minutes in the water. Those that did clung to hatch covers, planks, doors, and anything else that would float. Thomas said later that he found a six-foot long plank and clung to that.

Captain Anders Johnsen of the Norwegian bark *Ellen* was heading to Falmouth, England with a load of logs. At 1 a.m. Sunday he was standing on the quarterdeck with his helmsman, Gustav Jacobsen, when out of the darkness the men heard all around them the agonized cries of human voices. He roused his crew, put up lights, and began pulling survivors aboard. They pulled in the last survivor at 8 a.m. and continued searching until 11 a.m., and then they headed for Norfolk, Va.

Jane had been on the second lifeboat that transferred women and children from the stricken *Central America* to the brig *Marine*, and she feared for the life of her husband. According to a story in the *New York Herald*, the women had gathered in the cabin of the *Marine*, and around 9 p.m. a man entered and notified them that the *Central America* had gone down. "The steamer has sunk. I saw it go down, and every soul on her has gone to Davey Jones' locker," he said.

The women comforted each other with the knowledge that the men had life preservers and other items to keep themselves afloat, so they did not give up hope. Still, it would be hours before families would know the fate of their loved ones. Jane was taken to Norfolk with the other women and put up in the National Hotel. Thomas, who had been rescued by the *Ellen*, was also taken to Norfolk, but he and a group of other men boarded the night steamer *Louisiana* to Baltimore. Jane got word at the hotel that her husband had been saved, and, very relieved, she left the next morning for a reunion in Baltimore.

More than 400 passengers and crew members died in the sinking of the *Central America*. Thomas and Jane were one of only four couples to survive the disaster.

Thomas was one of the many heroes of the *Central America* tragedy. His experience as a sea captain aided greatly in keeping the ship afloat long enough for many passengers to be rescued. In appreciation of his efforts, the *Central America* New York Fund Committee presented him a large silver speaking trumpet engraved with mementos of the disaster. The inscription reads, "Presented to Captain Thomas W. Badger in token of their high appreciation of his conduct on board of the steamer *Central*

America, at the time of the loss of that ill-fated vessel. New York, May 17, 1858." The trumpet today is on exhibit at Ker Place in Onancock, Va., home of the Eastern Shore of Virginia Historical Society. A metal life preserver of his is on exhibit at the Mariners' Museum in Newport News, Va.

For more detailed information on the sinking of the Central America, including a narrative given by Thomas to *The New York Journal of Commerce*, see Appendix A.

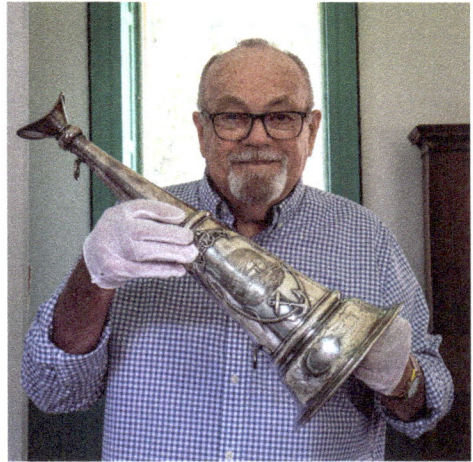

Author Curtis Badger with silver speaking trumpet.

This silver speaking trumpet was awarded to Captain Badger in recognition of his heroism during the sinking of the **Central America.**

Badger's Grand Central Park

Following their ordeal aboard the *Central America*, Thomas and Jennie took an extensive sabbatical on the Eastern Shore, visiting friends and family and taking the steamboat to Baltimore for shopping trips. But Thomas had business to attend to in California, and soon they returned. They bought a 10-acre tract on an inlet of San Francisco Bay in 1861, built a large home with many outbuildings, and planted extensive gardens.

This painting, **Residence of Capt. Thomas W. Badger, Brooklyn, from the Northwest,** *is an oil on canvas, 26.25x42 inches done circa 1871 by Joseph Lee. It is in the collection of the Oakland Museum of California, a gift of Lester M. Hale. Capt. Badger opened his amusement park on this property in 1872. It is now an industrail area in Oakland.*

Thomas owned several vessels which were engaged in commerce throughout the Pacific and elsewhere. Several were lost at sea, including the *Sunny South*, which had as a mate young George Martin, Thomas's nephew. Thomas expressed in letters to his brother his sadness over the loss of the young man, who had lived for a while with Jennie and him. In another letter he wrote of having a vessel trapped by ice in a river in Russia.

Thomas eventually tired of the life of a sea captain and turned his attention to his home and extensive gardens. He bought additional property in East Oakland, then known as Brooklyn Basin, and began construction of a large amusement park that included a bowling alley, restaurant, pavilion, baseball field, and a display of exotic plants and animals. Badger's Grand Central Park opened to the public on April 14, 1872 with 4,000 visitors attending.

The park, located near rail and ferry stations, was a great success, and at age 45 Thomas gave up the seafaring life to run the park. He sold his fleet of vessels, and he and Jennie concentrated their time and energy on the park. Still, Thomas did not completely give up his maritime interests. He served as pilot commissioner for the Port of San Francisco, and he also was a marine surveyor for Peoples Insurance Company.

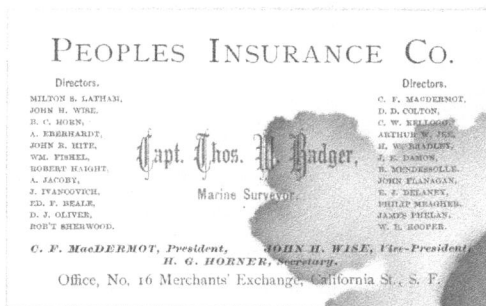

Thomas W. Badger's business card

The park was by all accounts a great success, and Thomas and Jennie were partners in the business. According to Mollie Conners, author of *Pioneering Women of Alameda County*, "Mrs. Badger led the vanguard of business women in the county. When her husband opened Badger's Park, she was his able assistant, and every day she accompanied him on his rounds. He looked after 'the talent' and she looked after the cash box. She was the first woman cashier in any of the activities of pioneer days in the county."

According to news accounts from the day, Badger's Park hosted a variety of events and activities. A picnic was held on September 9, 1875

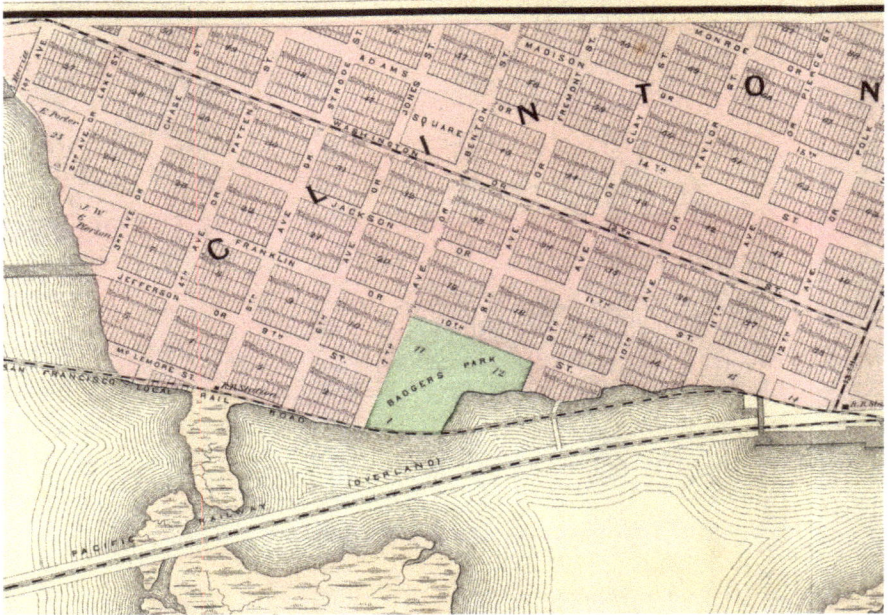

1878 map showing Badger Park

celebrating Admission Day, marking the 25th anniversary of statehood for California. Former president Ulysses S. Grant gave a speech to Civil War veterans in 1879. The *Daily Alta* (Northern) *California* reported on August 3, 1887 that "Carsten Carstens, a Swede, aged 23, died at 410 Beale Street on Monday, from injuries received by a fall from a trapeze at Badger's Park on July 23d. The unfortunate trapezist fell from the suspended bar and fractured his nose. Erysipelas ensued which finally caused death."

The park was located on the Brooklyn Basin side of Merritt Lake and boat races were often on the venue. Grandstands were built along the edge of the lake, and visitors could watch the regattas. The crews were made up of local club members, and although the rowers were amateurs, there often was some spirited competition.

On June 17, 1878 one of the club crews had to be rescued:

> *Promptly at two o'clock, a start was effected. The Ariels led,*
> *and, crossing the bow of the Pioneers, took the inside track. This*
> *advantage however they did not long maintain, being passed*

26

GRAND

May Festival

....AT....

Badger's Park,

....ON....

WEDNESDAY, MAY 1, '78,

FOR THE BENEFIT OF THE

School Children

....OF....

OAKLAND AND ALAMEDA

Premises to be a grand affair. The grounds are in splendid order, and appropriate decorations are going on for the occasion.

Walcott's full Brass Band of 15 pieces is engaged for the occasion, and it bids fair to be the grandest and pleasantest affair of the season.

All children under 12 years, accompanied by their parents, admitted free. All above 12 and under 15 years, 15 cents. Adults, 25 cents.

Times Copy.

BADGER'S
CENTRAL PARK,

Second Station above Broadway.

OAKLAND.

SPLENDID RESORT

For families to enjoy a sylvan retreat from all the dust and noise on the Fourth of July.

SATURDAY AND SUNDAY, JULY 5TH AND 6TH

First appearance of the great

JOHN C. COOKE,

Of London, who will appear in several of his unparalleled and Sensational Acts, including the

NIAGARA LEAP,
GREAT ÆRIAL ACTS,

Great Ærial Ascension to a giddy height, and his Miraculous Descent.

WILLIS' GRAND CONCERT BAND

Will be in attendance all day, and perform several choice operatic morceaux.

Several additions have already been made to the Menagerie.

Admission....................Twenty-five cents
Children...............................Ten Cents
Cars run to the Park.   j3-td

FOURTH OF JULY, 1878.

PRIZES
For Equestriennes.

CAPT. BADGER, OF BADGer's Park, offers to give two prizes—thirty ($30) dollars to the first and twenty ($20) dollars to second best, and fastest. Lady Rider out of four entries, the ladies to furnish their own horses and equipments. The race will be best in three, one mile and repeat. The track is in fine condition. Four times around makes one mile. This opportunity is offered to the ladies of Alameda county for one week.

None other but amateurs and respectable parties need apply. Address, or see in person, Thos. W. Badger, at the Park, in the forenoon and evening.

je15   THOS. W. BADGER.

Newspaper advertisements for Badger Park

27

by the Pioneers before the first stake-boat was reached. The Pioneers kept the lead until near home, when they unluckily "caught a crab," which mishap was taken advantage of by the Ariels, who made a spurt ahead and won the race by about six feet. The contest was very spirited throughout, and the winning crew was greeted with hearty cheers by the spectators assembled on the shore. A foul was claimed by the Pioneers, on the grounds that crossing their bow at the start, the Ariels did not allow the regulation two lengths of water between their boats.

An unusually heavy sea prevailed and was the occasion of a mishap for the California Theatre Club boat, which is too lightly built to stand the weather. Having shipped a quantity of water in making the start, it was swamped just after rounding the judge's boat on the first turn. A barge belonging to the Columbia Club promptly came to the assistance of the crew, who tenaciously clung to their oars until rescued.

Although the races were competitive, the events were social events, usually including picnics, music, and dancing. Here is a story from the *Daily Alta California* published on July 15, 1875:

The California Theatre Boat Club will hold a picnic and regatta today at Badger's Park, Oakland. Following is a list of the races to take place: First will be a single shell race between A. Trueworthy and Robert Harmon. This race is for the Junior championship of this coast. Second— A Whitehall race between Thomas Gossman and Walter Wallace. Third— The great six-oared barge race between Thomas Gossman, Charles H. Meatayer, Thomas Andrews, Peter Brown, J. Harrington, A. Trueworthy, John Kanter, and George Fenton, Coxswain. These contests will take place on the creek by the Park, and all will be enabled to get a full view from the stands. Music and dancing will make up the day's amusements.

Sometimes the park was the center of controversy, and it usually made the newspapers. One such incident occurred when the Cooks and Waiters Union, the Journeymen Bakers, and the Musicians' Union reported a very outrageous occurrence which happened at a recent picnic at Badger's Park. From the *Daily Alta California*:

> *It appears that a Union group which attended drank a keg of beer which, when they had finished it, they found to be from the United States Brewery, which is boycotted. Their horror and indignation was great, and they took steps to have the matter brought before the Council. Mr. Smith requested that the unfeeling proprietor of the park be asked to discontinue the sale of non-union beer.*

The activities at the park were covered regularly in the local newspaper, the *Daily Alta California*. Most of the stories involve picnics held by clubs and social groups, concerts, theater presentations, boat races, and other events. One story involved an event that didn't happen. Thomas Badger had contracted with an aeronaut to put on a balloon flight, but it turned out that the balloon refused to leave the ground, prompting the balloonist to sue his supplier. This article is from a May 1885 issue of the *Daily Alta California*:

> *Frank M. Knight, the aeronaut at Badger's Park, has sued Neville & Co. for $250. He alleges that in March last he purchased a hot air balloon from the defendants on their representation that it would ascend with the handicap of a man's weight. At the time, Knight was under contract with the proprietor of the Park to make an ascension, for which he was to receive $200.*
>
> *Relying on Neville & Co.'s guarantee, he did not test the air-ship until the date of the ascension. Then he found that it was barely capable of sustaining its own weight, and was totally incapable of carrying him heavenwards. He was consequently unable to fulfill his contract, and believes himself damaged in the amount named.*

Accounts vary as to how long the park stayed in operation. Some records say the park closed after five years because of complaints from neighbors, other accounts say the park was destroyed by fire. There was a fire in May 1885 which destroyed the pavilion, but it was rebuilt for the following season. Newspaper accounts list events taking place at the park as late as 1890, when the Butchers' Protective Association held its annual picnic there in May. And letters written from Thomas to John indicate that the park was in continuous operation for nearly 20 years.

Thomas writes in 1890 of turning down an offer of $50,000 for the park, and in May 1891 he writes that his nephew, Tom, had visited and drew a map of the park, which was one of his first jobs as a draftsman upon arriving in California. Thomas indicated in the same letter that he was actively making plans to sell the park. The area where Badger's Park was located is today a densely developed industrial tract.

The *Jane A. Falkenburg*

Thomas and Jennie sold the *Jane A. Falkenburg* when they were in Virginia in 1857 recovering from the *Central America* tragedy. But the vessel would play a lingering role in their lives. In December 1890 Thomas and Jennie were in their home overlooking the Oakland estuary when they noticed a barquentine making its way up the estuary seeking shelter from a storm. The captain anchored directly in front of their house, and they immediately recognized the vessel. It was the *Jane A. Falkenburg*, which they had not seen in 33 years.

Thomas died in Oakland on November 21, 1899. The *Oakland Tribune* noted upon his death that by coincidence, on the same day, "the ship *Jane A. Falkenburg*, laden with lumber from Puget Sound, was overturned and abandoned off the Mendocino Coast."

Jennie, after a prolonged illness, died less than three months later, on February 9, 1900, at age 65. Both were buried in Laurel Hill Cemetery in San Francisco alongside Charles A. Falkenburg. At the gravesite was a massive stone monument bearing a sculpture of the barquentine, *Jane A. Falkenburg*.

Letters Home

From Jennie to John

Thomas and Jennie got married in 1856, and she met the family the following year after the *Central America* tragedy. She seems to have had a quick wit and an engaging personality and was much loved by the family. In this letter she chides John about being on the "Old Bachelors List" if he doesn't soon get married. In the letter that follows this one, he proposes to Mary Frances, or Fannie, as he called her.

The phrases in Jennie's letter "just now enrolling" and "resorting to that as a means of raising funds" refer to the fact that Union agents were in San Francisco enrolling young men for the draft. Those drafted could purchase an exemption for $300. This also raises the question of whether the Captain's accident Jennie refers to was indeed accidental. Assuming he was righthanded, the finger he smashed was his trigger finger. If he had fought in the Civil War, he would not have fought on the side of the Union.

November 13, 1863

Dear Brother John,

Capt. (Thomas) *wrote you some twice ago but as yet we have not received any reply. I wrote Sister Vinia* (Lavinia) *not long since, hope that she has quite recovered from her illness. When we last heard from her she seemed quite desponding. Capt. met with quite an accident the other day getting the* Sunny South *ready for sea. In lifting a piece of timber he let it fall and mashed one of his fingers very badly. It hurt him so bad that it caused him to*

31

faint. It is the forefinger of his right hand. However, it is doing well now and the Sunny South *has sailed for Mexico.*

They are very busy here just now enrolling but I don't think that it will amount to much. I think that my husband will be exempt now that he has hurt his hand, and to tell the truth I would his arm be taken off than for him to be drafted. But they are resorting to that as a means of raising funds. Poor Creatures, how I pity them._____ have names I won't say. They may have me arrested. They are surely mean enough.

Well, where are you and what are you doing? Why don't you write us oftener? Rains have just set in, and last night we had the first shower and our grass looks beautiful this morning after it. Oh how I do wish that you could see our charming little home. I think it a perfect Eden on Earth and my husband thinks so too. I would be perfectly happy if I could get a good servant, but they are scarce here. We keep a man and woman and pay 30 dollars per month to the man and 25 to the woman. I am willing to pay that, but they are not good for anything. I keep changing all the time. I think that if we go home next spring I will venture to bring out a good black woman with us as they are the best help. If you have to give them the same they are better worth the money, and I would rather have a good black woman than to have one of those untidy Irish girls such as we are obliged to employ here.

When you see Sister Lizzie give her my love, and the girls the same, in fact all the family. How is Aunt Sallie and where is Cousin Joe and is he married yet? I am afraid that I will have to put you both on the Old Bachelors List if you don't get married before long. That likeness you sent me last is worse than the first. Don't go to that artist any more. It is all his fault. He makes you look so old. I will close with much love from us both.

I remain as ever your affectionate, Sister Jennie

THE PROPOSAL

John Wesley Badger married Mary Frances Tankard Floyd on November 15, 1865 when he was 33 years old and she was 25. They had

two sons, Thomas Norman and John Tankard. She was the widow of Richard Floyd and the daughter of J.W.S. and Susan Taylor Tankard. In this letter, written on October 19 and posted in New York, John says he wants to marry Fannie "as soon as I arrive." They were married less than a month later.

Dear Fannie,

As I promised to write you from this place you will not be surprised at receiving this. You will excuse my delaying it until I am ready for sea. Shall sail for home today. It may be that you will see me before this reaches you. I sincerely hope it may find you all in good health and you may rest assured that you are ever present in my mind. You are the center of all of my future hopes. I shall come home prepared to make you my bride and God grant that you may be a happy one. My preparations are not very expensive or extensive. I had rather have your assistance hereafter in purchasing what we may need in setting up our humble household. My fondest hopes are that we may be united as soon as I arrive.

Until then I remain yours most affectionately,

J. W. Badger

In February of 1866 John and Fannie made a shopping trip to New

York City to furnish their "humble household." They likely took John's ship *Panama* to New York loaded with freight, unloaded, and then began shopping for household items. Receipts show the purchase of an excelsior mattress from Truman and Tyler on Westminster Street, a serpentine bedstead from B.M. Cowperthwait in the Bowery, and assorted dishes and a gravy tureen from Richard Decker in Greenwich Street.

Unfortunately, their married life ended far too quickly. Fannie died six years after they were married at age 31. Her obituary says she died in Fredericksburg while visiting family and friends, and it says she had been in declining health for about a year. (See Appendix E)

New York, Feb'y 28th 1866

Mr J W Badger

Bought of **RICHARD DECKER**,
Importer and Dealer in China, Glass and Earthenware,
No. 219 GREENWICH STREET, between Barclay and Vesey Sts.

TERMS, CASH.

All Goods will be shipped per direction, and receipts taken for them, in good order, "and any damage" or loss that may occur in transportation will not be allowed.

1	Large Dish		1 75
1	Butter		1 00
6	Dishes 2/ 2/ 2/		4 50
1	Dz Plates		1 75
2	Food Dishes	17	2 50
2	Pea Dishes	57	1 25
1	Gravy Tureen		1 25
1	Dz Teas		2 25
		$16	25

Received Payment
R Decker
Rdecker

John in 1875 married Mary Sue Tankard, the daughter of Phillip Barraud Tankard and Elizabeth Rodgers Tankard. John and Mary Sue had six children: Elizabeth Frances (Bessie), George Henry, Julia Franklin, William Franklin, Margaret Julia (Maggie), and Susie Estelle.

THE CAPTAIN WANTS A BREWSTER BUGGY

Thomas wrote to his brother in 1866 and mentioned that if he happened to be in New York City over the next few months, he might send him a Brewster buggy. Apparently, the shipping business was lucrative in these months following the Civil War. The Brewster Carriage Co. was founded by James Brewster in 1810 in New York, and by 1827 had branches in New Haven and Bridgeport. In 1878 it won fame at the international carriage exhibition in Paris. The Brewster buggy was considered the Rolls Royce of horse-drawn carriages, and they are sought after today by collectors. In 1914 Brewster joined Rolls Royce and became the American distributor. Brewster manufactured an automobile of its own from 1915 to 1925 called the Brewster Knight. The company went out of business during the Great Depression and was sold at auction in 1937.

Sunny Side, Clinton, Alameda Co., May 28, 1866

John W. Badger,

Dear Brother,

I received your kind favor a few days since and was pleased to learn that you and yours was getting along as well as could be expected. You speak of dull times. That is what is the matter here and everywhere else, I believe. We are all tolerable well. Jennie has been complaining for some days. George Martin is here with us and has been since he arrived out here. Waiting the arrival of the brig Sunny South from Central America with a cargo of sugar and coffee, which is now due at this port. She will go to Japan the next voyage. He has not been able to procure a place worth having since his arrival, so I think it is best for him to go to sea. The farmers have very heavy crops this year here. We had a heavy rain on the 22nd this month. You mention about what you owe me, that need not trouble you. You owe me a very little anyhow.

You spoke of sending me a buggy. I do not wish you to put yourself out to send me a carriage, but if you should happen to be in New York this fall or summer and could spare the means as well as not, you might send me out a Brewster Buggy or a Watson make. This buggy is made in Philadelphia and is a very good, stylish carriage. But the Brewster of Broom St. New York is most generally preferred for its neat workmanship, good materials, and durability. Sometimes the above mentioned carriages are very high priced. In that case you might find some other maker that would do, but you would have to be careful as they only make them to sell. I want something good, durable, and stylish. My horses are small, so would not like too large a carriage, only two of us. I do not wish you to get this if it is inconvenient.

I don't know when I shall be able to come home, in fact I have very little desire since the war, it makes me sick to think of coming home and seeing the disturbance it has caused. We must all go in for Johnson. He may be able to save a remnant of the constituency yet. I hope the children are doing well. Give my regards to them all. You say something about being out here but I suppose you are comfortable where you are.

The brig Sunny South *has arrived all right and George went on board yesterday. He is well pleased with her and well he may be. She is in fine order and the finest vessel in port to her size. She will leave in ten days for Japan, Shangheigh China. That is the voyage for George. He is pleased.*

You must write me often, give my regards to Mr. Martin and family. My regards to your better half as well as yourself.

I remain your affectionate brother,

Thomas W. Badger

GEORGE MARTIN IS LOST IN THE SINKING OF THE *SUNNY SOUTH*

San Fransisco

May 25th, 1867

Dear Brother,

Your favor of March 13th came duly to hand and we were pleased to hear from you all. You also had received news of the loss of the brig Sunny South. *This is too true. She had never been heard from since she left Yokhama the 11th of September last. A sad thing for Mr. Martin and the girls as well as a great many others.*

I am about purchasing another vessel in the place of the Sunny South and possibly will go on a few voyages in her myself. In regards to the six hundred dollars you so kindly offer me, if I had it here I could possibly use it but you had better keep it as you cannot tell when you may want to use that amount. These times of Yankee ruin in your midst. Jennie and myself feel very bad about George, but we have all to go one after another and it appears to matter a very little which way we go. I have had a great many narrow escapes of my life since I first left home. (referencing the Central America *tragedy)*

I am in hopes that Mr. Martin lays no blame to me about George, as

I would have sent my own child on the same voyage and came neigh going myself as it was. The Captain was too good a man to turn out of the vessel, and much more experienced in those waters than me. It was a terrible typhoon, the worst that has visited the China Sea for a number of years. There were a number of vessels lost at the same time.

I wish you to write me how Mr. Martin is getting along. The note of George Bell is long ago settled and paid. In regards to my place at Red Bank I will send you sufficient proof of my citizenship soon.

In regards to selling the place I do not care to sell as the place was given to me by our father and mother. But you can live on or use the place as you please as though it were your own free from charges for rent and make just such improvements as you wish and if I ever come home to live then I will pay you for them.

I am pleased that you bought the Harrison place. It must have been cheap. About the carriage, it matters very little whether you send it or not. Enny time you happen to be in New York and can spare the money send it, but I wish you to suit your convenience about sending it. We have an old carriage and can get along with it for some time yet. Jennie and myself are enjoying tolerable good health. I should have written sooner but have been taking it from day to day. The time appears to fly, and a very little accomplished. I wish you to write me about all of our family's people and how things look like in our county.

We should like to pay you all a short visit in a few years. Jennie joins in love to you and your wife, hoping this will find you both enjoying good health. Write soon.

Your affectionate brother,

Thomas W. Badger

"THE INFERNAL RADICALS DIE HARD, HARSH OR EASY, BUT THEY DO NOT DIE FAST ENOUGH FOR ME"

Sept. 28, 1869

Dear Brother,

I wrote you some two months since and have not had a line from you or anyone else since. I feel a little alarmed at not having a letter from you. I hope that nothing has happened to you. It appears now the mails leave each day and run through in a week that we should hear from home more frequently. I am hoping all is well with you all.

Mr. Martin never writes me and I very seldom hear from Sister Lavenia. The Bell girls are silent, so we have no means of hearing from any of you. Jennie talks of going home most every day but said she cannot go without me and I am so employed that I cannot leave for some time to come. I have just accepted a situation as Marine Surveyor for the Peoples Insurance Co. of this place which I have to give my attention a few hours each day.

Western Pacific is now building their railroad past my property in Clinton, which of course has not depreciated the value of property in that vicinity. Money has been remarkably scarce here for the last two months. Everything has been to a standstill as a consequence. Business no doubt will soon rally again. Jennie and myself are in pretty good health and hope this finds you and yours enjoying the same good blessings.

You must write us at your earliest convenience as we are anxious to hear from you and tell the girls to drop us a few lines frequently. I often note in the papers about your state political troubles. The infernal radicals die hard, harsh or easy, but they do not die fast enough for me.

Your affectionate brother,

Thomas W. Badger

The Railroad is Coming

January 31, 1870

Dear Brother,

Yours of December 25th was kindly received and contents noted. I am pleased to hear that you and our family are in pretty good health. I have just

39

got clear of a very bad cold which I had for several weeks. The weather is fine now and has been for the last two weeks. We have had ample rain in this neighborhood, but the southern counties are suffering for the want of rain. The cattle have commenced dying from consequence of their having no grass.

Business is very dull here this winter, money scarce. Freighting is extremely dull. My bark is now in Chile. Had a good freight down. It looks doubtful for a good freight back. Sugars are low in this port and a large stock on hand, in consequence I fear they will not ship large from Peru. The ship Invento, which I own a part of, is now coming in with a load of salt.

The railroad is now about completed in front of my residence. We can take the cars three hundred yards from my house and ride right through to Baltimore or New York. Which trip I hope to be able to take this summer. I am trying to arrange my matters with that view. I have not sold any real estate and do not expect to. I shall hold on to my land here unless I get big prices.

I am building a house dwelling to rent. We can rent houses very readily to family of business men. It being only forty-five minutes to the city of San Francisco. This building will cost me $2,500 when completed and will rent for from $45 to $50 per month and at the same time the land will probably increase in value. I have one house cost $1,600 two year ago. Rents steady for $35 per month and another house cost $1,200 and rents for $25 per month. I only mention this to show you the prorate of investment. Property certainly is low in your section of the country.

I saw your old friend Robinson the other day. He lives in the city. When I talked with him he inquired after you. He is getting very old. I do not know whether the old man has much means or not. I think he has not much. He had a son in the Federal Army all the war with Grant. The old man is very conservative.

Everything is much the same as usual in this city. The Insurance business is dull as every other business. I am glad to see the young people get married. It shows that they are getting pretty well settled.

My love to you all and particularly to my boy Tom (his nephew, Thomas N. Badger).

Write me often and let me know how you and everybody else is.

Your affectionate brother,

Thomas W. Badger

"BUSINESS IS WELL OF ALL BRANCHES"

June 7, 1870

Dear Brother,

Yours of the 27ᵗʰ came duly to hand and contents noted. You appeared despondent about the elections. The Negroes have it everywhere. Negroes went to the polls here today and voted. It is better here as there. Jennie and myself are in pretty good health. Hope this will find you and yours the same.

Tell my boy Tom I will ride his colt when I come. Jennie is talking of coming ahead of me as several of our friends are soon to leave for the East.

I wish in answer to this, you will let us know how the boats run and the best way to get home from Baltimore. Also where is the best place to put up in Baltimore. You will see us sometime in the summer. Business is well of all branches. Real estate has deals and so far profit exceeds loss.

Your affectionate brother,

Thomas W. Badger

JENNIE TAKES THE WESTERN PACIFIC TO BALTIMORE

March 13, 1871

Dear Brother,

I wrote you two weeks since have not had a line from you for a long time. Jennie and myself are in pretty good health. Hope you and yours are enjoying the same good blessing.

Jennie will leave here (on the Western Pacific Railroad) *for Baltimore Monday morning, March 27ᵗʰ if nothing unusual happens. She will go on*

41

the first boat for Pungoteague after her arrival in Baltimore. Once at Mr. Martin's then she can reach you all. She will probably stay at the Fountain Hotel where we lived so long (probably after the sinking of the Central America). Do not know whether the proprietors are the same or not.

I cannot come with her at present. May come in the summer. This trip was only made up a few evenings ago. We were visiting our neighbor, Judge Standley, when Mrs. Standley spoke of her intentions to visit Wilmington, North Carolina, her's as well as the Judge's native place. So they accompany one another all the way to Baltimore. So there is no necessity of anyone going to meet her as she is somewhat acquainted with Baltimore.

Martha Bell is somewhere near Baltimore. If you drop her a line she would call and see Jennie at the Hotel, or any other friends who happen to be in Baltimore. They will be pretty sure to be there the 5ᵗʰ of April. Jennie will have no trouble in getting along as she will have little or no baggage, which is the best way to travel in the Western Pacific cars.

My suit has not come to a trial yet. Maybe some time first. Can't force these matters. Business of all kinds are dull here. The grapes are only tolerable if we have late rains, if not the grapes will be a failure. Shipping is dull. I have a vessel that I think is frozen up in the Amur River, Russia.

If you write to Jennie, address Mrs. Capt. T. W. Badger, Fountain Hotel. I do not know whether the wires extend down your way or not.

Jennie may lay over one boat in Baltimore if she feels fatigued. I wish it was so I could come with her, but impossible for the present. I hope to get matters in a better shape soon.

My love to all. Write soon.

Your affectionate brother,

Thomas W. Badger

ON RED BANK LANDING

February 17, 1874

Dear Brother,

Jennie received a few lines from you, also did I. In regards to Mr. Martin's place on Pungoteague Creek, I have no notion of buying any land in Virginia or any other place. The fact is I am land poor. It takes all I can make to pay the expenses on any land here. I never was shorter of money than I am at present. Since I returned I have laid out about $3,000 which I had to borrow. I will not be able to take in any money until April. The grading of street around my place (the park) *has been very expensive.*

I would not like to see Mr. Martin sacrifice his property, and if he can hold on until I may be in a position to help him. Keep me posted.

In regards the place where you live, I always intended to give it to your two boys and if I should come back to live I would pay you for all the improvements. You can think over the matter and write me more fully what you wish and the shape you wish to put it in. I urge you to write to me all the business letters and Jennie the friendly letters. Address my letters N.E. Corner Bush & Kearny Street, San Francisco and Jennie's to East Oakland, Cal.

We were one week in New York, very expensive place. Went out on the Erie Railroad via Niagara Falls through Canada and in Detroit, Michigan stayed 4 days and in Chicago one day. I passed the Sierras, plenty of snow, got down in the valley sunshine.

Your affectionate brother,

Thomas W. Badger

STATE CONVENTION COMING UP

San Francisco

Jan. 28ᵗʰ, 1875

Dear Brother John W. Badger

Yours of the advice of receipt of Coupons and contents noted. I am sorry to learn that you was not well. I had heard of Henry Dunton's death. Poor fellow. His time in this world was short.

My business is dropping off. I have done well this year, but it all goes into property. I have had about 1200 feet of front property graded and curbed. This done at our expense of 1,600 dollars.

Our state convention comes off tomorrow. I have the honor to be a delegate from Alameda County, one of several chosen by the democrats of the County. Jennie and myself is in tolerable good health.

Hope you and yours are the same. Write to me about Lavinia and Elizabeth.

Love to all. Write often.

Thomas W. Badger

Jennie Doesn't Like the Park Business

San Francisco

February 2, 1875

Dear Brother John,

Your kind letter was duly received. Was glad to learn that both yourself and the children were well. I am glad to learn that you have been having such nice times with the young Tommy.

Christmas was dull with us. My house was all upset and is so still, and more, I got quite a severe fall on Christmas night. I fell head-first down a whole lot of steps just outside our kitchen door. Capt. says I had a narrow escape.

I hurt one of my fingers in putting out my hand to break the fall. I am thankful that I was not crippled. I tell Capt. that was my Christmas present.

Your letter to Captain he did not get for some time after I got your last. It is more direct to send your letters to Oakland as that mail we can get every night as Capt. does not go to the city regular. In regards to Capt. buying Mr. Martin's place, he says he had no such idea, and that if he did he had no funds to purchase it as it has been slack with him for some time, and in fact ever since he opened his place to the public.

Though I do wish that he could sell our place there. I would bid goodbye to the dear public and being a public servant. I positively despise this business. It is only fit for Germans as Sunday and Monday is all the same to them. With me it is different. I do not believe in any kind of amusements on the Sabbath. It is the Lord's day and I was taught to respect it. And while on this business it is impossible. There is nothing but care and work all the time in such business, and I am sick and tired of it. Have been at it almost four years now. This coming season will be the fourth. Capt. says he hopes this will be the last season he will carry it on. I hope and pray it may be. Will close with much love to you and the children.

Your affectionate sister,

Jennie

In August the Captain wrote to his brother about hosting a picnic for the Pioneers to celebrate Admission Day. Admission day is the celebration of California becoming the 31st state on September 9, 1850. Admission Day is still a state holiday. The Pioneers were a group of early settlers who were in California prior to 1850. The modern day Society of Pioneers is a non-profit organization with membership open to anyone who had descendants in California prior to 1850. The headquarters is at 300 Fourth Street in San Fransisco.

THE PIONEERS PICNIC

San Francisco

August 28th, 1875

John W Badger

Dear Brother,

Yours informing me of the payment of the Fort Madison Bond Cuponds (coupons) is received and contents noted. We are all well. Hope you and the family the same. My busy season is fast coming to a close. Henry is still with us. He is improving slowly.

The Pioneers have a picnic at my place Sept 9th Admission Day.

San Francisco is now today undergoing the greatest excitement which has taken place in several years. Three of the largest banks in this place have failed and closed doors this day, and mining stocks have dropped very low. The whole has a demoralizing effect on the people. I thank God I owe little or nothing, and it can't hurt me much.

I wish you to secure for me from William LeCato ten gallons of the best peach brandy. Also, ten gallons of apple brandy. Write me how Mrs. Martin is getting along. Tell Tommy to catch me some marsh hen birds, and keep them for me. Also, reed birds (bitterns) *and quail.*

Give love to all

I miss you

Affectionate Brother

Thomas W Badger

The Eastern Shore was well known in the 19th Century for its peach brandy. Most farms included large orchards and grape arbors. Peach brandy and scuppernong wine were favorites.

CALIFORNIA POLITICS AND PEACH BRANDY

January 25, 1876

Dear Brother,

I have been promising myself to write you for a long time, but have put it off until now. I have been in hot water ever since the first of September. Politics and an attempt to open a street through my park has been the subject of annoyance. But I have survived through both. Last night the City Council decided not to open the street in question, and this morning I take my seat as one of the Pilot Commissioners, having been commissioned by Governor Irwin. I was in the State Convention that nominated him last fall. My name was sent in to the Senate for confirmation. Every man in that body voting for me. W. J. Timmin has been a good friend of mine.

The Legislature is in session. I have driven up to Sacramento off and on for the last three weeks. Thank God I am through.

Timmin is in the Senate, his wife is with him. She is an elegant lady. They visited us last Christmas, also a man and his family by the name of McGilbray, all from Weaverville. Dr. Teash, Burch and wife lived here. Burch ....good fellow. They all know you and Joseph D.

I am busy fitting up my place (the park) *for summer work. My health has not been good this winter. I do not think I can come home this summer.*

About my peach brandy, I would like for you to ship it by express from Baltimore as soon as you can. You will have to put the keg inside of another keg or inside a case to guard against people drawing the brandy off. Otherwise, they will draw the brandy and fill it up with water. In regard to the property of mine where you live, I am willing for your boys to have that place, and am willing to give you a deed for the same. Providing that I can have the privilege of building a house and occupying one half of the field where your house now stands during mine and Jennie's life. Providing we will so do in case I should close out all my interest in this state and we came to the Atlantic Coast to live. I wish to have a summer house and that would be the place I would want a house.

William Bell is with us from Louisiana. Henry is on the street cars, getting 2 ½ dollars per day and likes it well. Much love to all.

Thomas W. Badger

A DUEL IN EASTVILLE

In March 1878 a duel, or shootout, in Eastville apparently made the newspapers in San Francisco. It involved two young men from prominent families and a $20 debt. The men were Major S. Pitts and Albert P. Thom. Pitts was killed in the shooting, and Thom was badly wounded with a bullet in the jaw. He survived, however, and went on to become a prominent attorney in Norfolk.

47

March 30, 1878

Dear Brother,

I see by this morning's paper a duel took place at Eastville between Thomas and Pitts. Both killed. Do I know the parties? Write me the particulars.

I shall have a busy day tomorrow Sunday. Matters beginning to look bad here. There has been a party started made up of the tail end of both the old parties. They can make it pretty rough. We expect a little trouble.

Jennie and myself in tolerable health. Hope you and yours enjoying good health. The State legislature adjourned on Monday. Write soon. Let me know how you all are. Much love to all.

I remain your affectionate brother, Thomas W. Badger

TERRAPIN DINNER IS VERY FINE

San Francisco, January 23rd 1884

John W. Badger

Northampton Co, VA

Dear Brother,

Received on the 11th the fish and terrapins which is very fine. All in fine order. I had a terrapin for dinner the same day. I gave Judge Wright two terrapins. He is an old Virginian having lived in Williamsburg when a young man. I have now several mess of the fish and they are fine. We thank you much for the kind present. They came right to my door only ten days in transit.

Jennie and myself are in tolerable good health. Hope you and yours are under the same blessings.

In reference to the property where you live. I hardly know what to say. I certainly intended that property to go to you or your children after my death and Jennie is willing that it should now .... Should I sell out here, I would like to come home and live the balance of my days. I have no particular love for this country. Over one half of the people here are foreigners. Things are looking very blue here at present, though has been no rain and no doubt the grapes will be thin. There is at present time five millions worth of ship property in this port (with) nothing to do, and will not be for 15 months of time. There is plenty of money, but no one cares to invest in real estate. The rate of interest is now from 5 to 9 percent per annum. I was in hopes to sell real estate enough to pay up my debts, but I fear it will be some time.

I can with economies pay my taxes and interest, but it is all I can do. I hate to sacrifice my property that I have held for so long. I will run the Park this summer. Jennie dislikes it very much, and so do I on her account. We have some fine friends here, but they would not keep me here. It is true the coast is filling up with people, and things are gradually improving, but it is no better than any of the Old Atlantic States.

If it could be arranged in a deed to you, reserving about 6 acres out to the south of the house, and after Jennie's and my death have it revert to the holders of the place with improvements. In the mean time you have the use of the land unless I come home and built on it which would improve the whole. Think on this, and write me fully. Whatever you do keep it to yourself, and address to my office in San Francisco N.E. corner of Market and Kearny in c/o E. Sheyers. Write soon. Love to all. What is Lavinia's address, so I can write. Love to all relatives and friends,

Thomas W. Badger

RAILROAD EXCURSIONS TAKE BUSINESS FROM PARK

July, 31st, 1884

Dear Brother,

It has been a long time since I had a line from you; however, I believe I am in your debt. I was briefly nearby one month prior to the 4th of July making big preparations for a celebration at the park and expecting to make at least $1,000 for myself. But there appears always something to spoil my pie. The people had three holidays, Friday, Saturday, Sunday, which opportunity does

49

not happen often for this business. Now there are some half dozen railroads running from here to all points on the continent – north, south and the interior that get up group excursions, so consequently I was left with only a couple hundred dollars for all my trouble and the risk of $1,000 dollar exhibitions. However, I gave great satisfaction to those that did attend. This has been the worst season I have ever had. It rained all the Sundays left in the month. I think the Salvation Army has us. If we can just survive from the weather we have had this summer.

Jennie and myself are in tolerable good health. Hope this will find you and yours the same. Mr. William Bell's family is living in one of my houses which they pay 23 dollars rent. They appear to be nice people. Mrs. Bell is a very pleasant, old lady. He is working at Mariposa, and consequently not with his family much.

Jennie sends her love to you and all of the children. I was in hopes that things would start up here, but very little moves in real estate.

Write soon and let me know how matters are with you.

Your affectionate brother,

Thomas W. Badger

The Park Burns

Thomas claimed that the 1884 season was the worst he had ever had at the park, and for 1885 he leased the park to M.V. Stevens. Unfortunately, early in the 1885 season the pavilion at the park was destroyed by fire. The Captain rebuilt the pavilion and continued operating it on his own for at least five more years. The *Daily Alta California* reported on the fire in its May 2, 1885 issue:

> *DISASTROUS FIRE IN OAKLAND*
> *At 9:35 o'clock last evening a fire broke out in the kitchen of the restaurant in the Pavilion at Stevens' Park, formerly known as Badger's Park, Oakland. The flames spread rapidly,*

and in a few minutes the entire Pavilion was in flames, and the building, which cost about $7,500, was burned to the ground and is a total loss. The windmill and water-tank adjoining were also destroyed.

The property burned is fully covered by insurance. The contents of the building, including a balloon and the wardrobe in the performers' room are a complete loss. The park, which is owned by Captain Thomas W. Badger and leased by M. V. Stevens, has been engaged for picnics by a large number of societies. May-Day festivities were held there during the day yesterday, but when the fire broke out all were gone except Mr. Stevens' daughter and the employees of the place.

Mr. Stevens suffers heavily and is caused great inconvenience. He but recently leased the Park from Mr. Badger. The cause of the fire is unknown, but it is supposed to be the work of incendiaries, as the fire did not break out until after the Park and Pavilion had been closed. It is stated that the Pavilion will be rebuilt at once. The total loss is estimated at about $12,000.

THE CAPTAIN IS SELLING THE PARK

February 26, 1890

Dear Brother,

It has been a long time since I wrote you, but there is no cause and a very little excuse for not writing oftener. I received your two letters all right last November. Well, we have had a horrible winter, 40 inches of rain up to now and likely to have 4 or 5 inches more. It has caused extensive damage all through the state and in fact

CAPT. THOS. W. BADGER

51

all along the coast from San Diego to Puget Sound. The farmers cannot get wheat in the ground because it is so soft that a horse can't pull the plow. It has been very sickly all over. Hundreds of old pioneers of this state have died. Each day tells of someone going to His long home. It makes me feel bad. I feel that I am getting old and will have to go sooner or later.

I am anxious to sell off enough property to pay up all my indebtedness, but the market has been quite unsatisfactory. But I shall endeavor to dispose of the Park property this summer even at a reduced price. The lease expires next year. The property is worth what I ask, $60,000, but I really have not had an offer for much over $40,000. The other property outside of the Park is all right. That is in shape to leave even for one year. There is one other thing connected with the park that required my presence. Some portion of the land, though smaller, floods and I reclaimed it. This piece has no chain of title, but is in my name now and the title is good, and has never been disputed. But purchasers are shy.

We see a very little of Mr. Bell in fact. We all have had to keep close this winter. They no doubt are doing well. I have not gone to San Francisco in over a month. In fact I will not go out evenings as we have to keep two fires going all winter, night and day. The undertakers have had a fine business this winter.

This is a great Country and Republic. This city is feeding one to two hundred tramps a day. Brick layers get $6.00, house carpenters $3.50 to $4.00, laborers $2.00 to $2.50 per day. The tramps come to the back door for sympathy, so I ask them to work, or if they want work. I offer $2.00 or $2.50 a day, and will do nothing for that.

Well, I hope this finds you and the family well and in good spirits. Jennie sends her love to all. Love to Lavinia, Julia, and all friends white and black. Write soon.

Your affectionate brother forever,

Thomas W. Badger

Undated letter, written in the spring of 1890

Dear Brother,

I wrote you some months since and have not had a line from you for a long time. I have very little to write about, but it being a very fine spring Monday morning, I decided to drop you a line. My health has improved and both myself and Jennie's health is pretty good. Hope this will find you and yours enjoying the same good blessing. This has been the roughest winter ever known here. I hope it will be good for the country generally, but everything is flat just now, a great stagnation in all business. The farmers have not been able to get their crops in, and it is a very late spring.

The people who visited this coast from the East are not so favorably impressed with the climate this winter. This may interfere with the general immigration of permanent settlers, which may cause real estate to drag, but is has dragged so long we have rather gotten used to it. There is, and has been, lots of opportunities to exchange city property for farming lands. Had I seized this opportunity offered me two years ago, it would have been well for me. Values for land in the valleys and farming land in the San Francisco area have almost doubled.

Do you not recollect Judge Roseboro? He was on the bench at Weaverville at the time you were there. He is a pretty old man, and he practices law here now. He and Jennie are great friends.

Is Mary Tankard's husband and children well fixed? How many children did she leave? Let me know. Has Rogers any children, and if so how are they fixed? I believe Henry has no children living. I suppose Lavinia is upset by this. Tell her to write to Jennie and me. I hope you will have a favorable year. Love to Sister Lizzie. Have not seen any of the Bells this winter. I have been out but little this winter. Of course you know Mary has been in New Orleans all winter. She is a fine looking lady and quite smart. She has a good education. Love to the boys and to your family and all our friends. Hope to hear from you soon.

I remain your affectionate brother forever,

Thomas W. Badger

So Rich Yet So Poor

August 28, 1890

Dear Brother.

It has been a long time since I wrote you, and you may think it wrong, but the only reason for such a delay is that I have been waiting to write you some good news, but in vain. Things were never duller than at present. Jennie is well and devoting her spare time to the furthering of the church while I am trying to make both ends meet.

I got food poisoning and was under the doctor's charge until now. I am better now. I am troubled quite often in my head with a sort of vertigo. But I hope to be able yet to square up the masts of my business. If we had another overland railroad our property would readily advance, so we hope this event will soon take place. Oakland never has had more improvements underway, but notwithstanding real estate, all else is very quiet. I had an offer for the park property the other day of $50,000. My asking price is $60,000. I asked if they would split the difference, but they declined. I think within one year I will get $60,000. I have not sold one other property since I wrote. I have had to pay for street improvements this year, over $10,000, to say nothing of taxes. The park is open and running every day through November. I am all this time grading and filling the low lands about the park. Each load of earth costs something, and still we manage to live sans servant. I chop the wood.

Jennie gets mighty tired of it sometime. So rich, yet still so poor. We have a Chinaman to come in and do a half days washing once in a while and we pay 75 cents. However, I am cheerful. Jennie at times is saddened as the old Californians are dropping off. I go to a funeral about once a month. Dr. Merritt, you may have heard me mention his name, has done a great deal for Oakland. I have been somewhat associated with him since the early days. He was a bachelor and left one million dollars. I think this city will be a large place and eagerly sought for business. It abounds with schools both public and private and churches of all denominations, but the officials are entirely too extravagant and going too fast with improvements, and causing the taxes to go too high.

I often think of you all. I am sorry for the Dunton children. God's will be done.

I hope this will find you and all your family in good health and the boys doing well. Give them my best wishes, as well as all friends, white or black. I have not heard a line from Lavinia. How is she and her son? John, write me soon. Let me know how you are and how you are getting along. I hope to be able to help you a little soon.

I remain your affectionate brother forever,

Thomas W. Badger

Thomas Norman Badger

Thomas Norman Badger, Uncle Tom to my father's generation, was born at Red Bank Landing on December 2, 1867. His parents were John Wesley and Mary Francis (Fannie) Tankard Badger. His younger brother, John Tankard, was born on July 26, 1870 at Red Bank, and the two remained close throughout their lives. John Tankard was known to everyone as Tank, possibly because the family realized there were a confusingly large number of "Johns" among them. Fannie died less than a year after Tank was born, and on May 6, 1875 John Wesley married Mary Sue Tankard. He and Mary Sue would have six more children, and the eight siblings would grow up to be very close, as the following letters attest.

Since the first edition of this book was published in 2014, more letters from Thomas Norman Badger have been found in the estate of Margaret Badger Dunton and her heirs, principally Joan Dunton Duer McMath and her husband, Ned McMath. The entire collection of letters and photographs has been donated to the Eastern Shore of Virginia Heritage Center in Parksley.

Tom lived for most of his adult life in California, and the new letters document his early years and the pathway that would lead him westward, much like his uncle. Tom left the family farm and enrolled at Virginia Military Institute in Lexington in 1883 when he was sixteen years old. He studied civil engineering and drafting, but he apparently left VMI before getting a degree. His last letter home from VMI was written in July 1895, and subsequent letters came from Washington, D.C., where he had gone to work for the Coast Survey, and then from Philadelphia, where a job with the Pennsylvania Railroad lured him ultimately to seek his fortune out west.

Thomas N. Badger with his drafting equipment

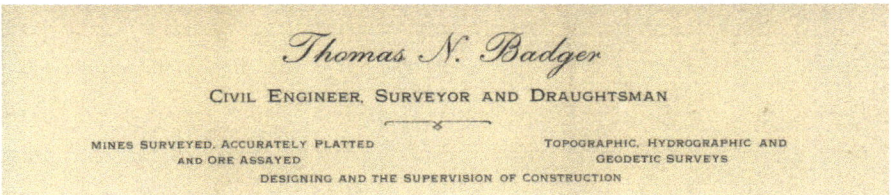

Thomas N. Badger's letterhead from 1899

Virginia Military Institute

Lexington, Va.

January 23, 1883

My dear Father,

I received your letter containing the two checks and answered it a few days ago after I had received it, but I suppose my letter must have been lost. I have since received one from Eddie Tankard informing me of the death of little Julia. Poor little thing. When I left she was running about, smiling and playing and little did I think that I would never see her again on Earth, but God in his providence has seen fit to remove her from this world of sin and trouble, and I think it is a great consolation to know that such as her do inherit the Kingdom of Heaven. (Julia was Tom's half-sister.)

I have also received a letter from Cousin Mary Tankard and she asked me why I act so indifferent towards you by not writing to you. Let me assure you my dear father that if I had acted indifferently toward you it was certainly not intentional, but I may have faults that I cannot see, I know that I have not always treated you as I ought to have done, but God knows that I love you, and I do ask you and pray to God to forgive me for all my misdoings. Nothing on Earth gives me more pain than to know what sacrifices you have made to keep me in school, and I am willing to stop at any time and go to work. I would have answered your letter immediately after I received it, but at that time my examinations were going on and they took all my time.

I know of nothing of interest to write you about except that they are still having trouble here at the institute. A few nights ago, someone removed a cannon from the gun shed and loaded it with a ten-pound dumb-bell and tried to fire it at the Garrison, and had it gone off it would probably have blown up the barracks and likely killed a great many of the cadets. They have a regular organized band here in this school that goes by the name of Mollies who are always up to something of that kind.

I must now bring my letter to a close. Please write of times and long letters as I hear very little from home and receive very few letters.

From your loving son,

T.N. Badger

SUMMER SCHOOL IN LEXINGTON

V.M.I., Lexington, Virginia

July 28, 1885

My dear Father:

Your letter received and I take the earliest opportunity to answer. I have decided to spend the summer here, as I feel it will be much better for me to remain here. My report is not as good as it might have been, although I did about as well as I could expect under the circumstances. In regard to failing an examination on English, I will say that more than half of my class will have to stand a new examination, and I do not think I will have any trouble getting through. If I remain here next year, I will have a much better chance to study and take a good stand than I did this year and I assure you that I can, and will, but nothing pains me more than to know you have to work so hard, and I want you to consider well before you undertake to send me here another session. I enclose a list of my expenses for last session, and the principle part of my expenses for the next session. I know of nothing else of interest to write you and must now bring my letter to a close. Write soon.

Your devoted son,

T.N. Badger

This is the last letter we have from Tom during his college career at VMI. He apparently left before receiving a degree, but he was sufficiently prepared to go to work as an engineer or draftsman. He seems to have applied himself more enthusiastically to the engineering courses rather than to those in English. After returning home for a few months to teach school, Tom went to Washington D.C where he went to work making maps for the Coast Survey. The job did not seem to be a good fit.

Bad News Is Worse Than No News

Washington, D.C.

November 11, 1889

My Dear Father,

Your letter received some time ago and I expect you are beginning to think it about time I had given you an answer. I have had very little to write about, or I might say that I have had no good news to write and accepting the old axiom, "bad news is worse than no news at all" I have consequently delayed in answering.

The treatment I have received from the chief of our fort since I came back here has caused me to become very much dissatisfied with my place. He stole $6 of my regular pay for the month of September so that I only received $54 for that month, and I came very near giving up the place as I found that the only way I could get my money. He consoled me by telling me he would raise my pay $5 from December to the end of the fiscal year. You may imagine how consoling such a statement was. Well, I may give up this place at any time. The only thing that has kept me from stopping is the position in which I have placed myself by investing all of my own money and going in debt besides. It has learned me a lesson That I won't forget soon, but if I am lucky enough to finish this month without accident to myself or team I will at least be out of debt. I have now commenced work with a view to getting in the office and am going to stand a civil service examination some time in January and hope I may succeed in getting it.

Have you heard from Aunt Lavinia lately? Give me a long letter as soon as convenient as I am anxious to hear from you all.

Your devoted son,

T. N. Badger

A January 19, 1890 letter reports that Tom was still working for the Coast Survey but he was not happy with the position. Nothing else was mentioned about taking a civil service exam, but by the spring of 1890 Tom had left Washington for Philadelphia, where he went to work for Pennsylvania Railroad and living in an apartment at 910 North 7th Street.

WORKING ON THE RAILROAD

April 8, 1890

My dear Father,

I think I may say that I am giving satisfaction in my work. I have just finished a large and rather difficult drawing, a map of the road from Baltimore to Odenton. The original drawing was about one hundred feet long and drawn to a scale so that one inch on the drawing represented one hundred feet of road. I had to take this drawing and make a map of the same portion of road i.e. from Baltimore to Odenton to be only ten feet long. That is to say one inch on my map would represent 1,000 feet of road. It looked like a right smart task when I started out on it as I had never done any of that kind of work before, but I put my shoulder to the wheel and soon caught on to the system and finished the job up in a satisfactory manner. (The railroad line between Baltimore and Odenton is still in service and is used by Amtrak.)

When I came here I took the place of a young man who was discharged the day I commenced work. I have not been able to learn exactly why he was discharged but suppose it was because he was incompetent.

Well, I am standing on my own merits here, if I stand at all, for I don't know a soul connected with the company except Mr. Cummings and he holds a minor position and I don't suppose he has a great deal of influence. Mr. Cummings, you know, is the gentleman through whom I made application. He has been very kind to me and I think wrote to the assistant chief engineer in my behalf. The men I am thrown with here in the office are very pleasant gentlemen. My chief especially is quite a contrast to the one I was with in the Coast Survey.

I am going to devote about all of my time to my work in the office for *the first month or two. If they keep me here and raise my pay, all so good and well, if they don't want me I am still satisfied. I don't intend to work long for $50 if there is any way to do better. I know of a man by the name of Bell who runs a large private surveying office, expect he is the one you speak of. Will be glad if you will write me Cousin George Bell's address. If there is anything I can do for you, let me know.*

Your son,
T.N. Badger

At this point, Thomas was 23 years old and still searching for a rewarding and challenging career. He was gaining experience as a civil engineer and working on a variety of projects. He seemed to enjoy the people he worked for and worked with, but he was not satisfied with the pay and the chances for advancement. One of the benefits of working for PRR was that he could get a railroad pass and in a few hours be back home in Northampton County to visit relatives.

VISITING AUNT LAVINIA

May 18, 1890

My Dear Father:

Your letter and postal received. I wish I could see Aunt Lavinia and John when they pass through the city but suppose it will be almost impossible for me to do so, but I can get a pass and go home any Saturday. Let me know when they will be at your house and will try to come down.

I am back with my old instruments again, at work in the field, am under a very pleasant gentleman and my work is not as hard as it was in Washington. The only objection I have to find with my place here is the pay I am getting and am sorry to say that. I don't see much prospect of advancement. There are two other young men on the party besides myself. They have been at work for a year or two and are getting the same pay that I am. So you see that I can't make up my mind to stay with the PRR with such a future as that ahead of me, but in the meantime I am gaining valuable experience and am not sorry that I came here. I am now learning practical work. Our work is about six miles out and we are building a long bridge just beyond the low water mark of the Schuylkill River. Write as soon as you can.

Your son,

T.N. Badger

Tom's next letter to his father is from California, dated July 26, 1891, so he decided at this point to seek his fortune in the American west, probably encouraged by his uncle Capt. Thomas W. Badger, who at this time was a successful shipping merchant and owner of an amusement park in Oakland. It is likely that Tom's uncle helped him secure an engineering job with the railroad in Fresno. Thomas W. and his brother John had a friend, Wiley Tinnin, who was a merchant and lawyer in Fresno and served in the state legislature.

This letter is from Wiley Tinnin to John Badger in Red Bank. Apparently, the two men had been friends during John's time in California, and this letter seems to indicate that John was in the mercantile business with Tinnin. Capt. Tom took his nephew to meet the influential businessman and politician, and this letter to John indicates that Tom did not follow up on an invitation to make a subsequent visit.

Wiley J. Tinnin

Tinnin & Mann

Attorneys and Counselors at Law

420 California Street, Rooms 12 and 13

Elevator 100 Leidesdorff St

San Francisco, Cal. Dec. 23rd, 1890

Friend Badger,

I met your son and Capt. Badger on Market Street a few days past and am pleased to receive your letter recalling old times and pleasant friends and associates.

Since our separation and the closing out of our mercantile business, I have sought other fields of employment among them law and politics. I have held several elective offices through the Democratic party and have canvassed the state several times in the interest of the party. I am often reminded of the many old residents of Trinity County for when on these tours through the state it makes no difference how small the town, I always find some old acquaintance from Trinity to greet me and talk over the days from 1851 up. Weaverville, where John lived, is in Trinity County.

I am the appointee of Mr. Cleveland as the surveyor of the Port of San Francisco, and served there until Mr. Harrison demanded my place for a Republican. It was the hottest place I ever got into for the reason of the Chinese troubles and a smuggling ring which had been under my predecessors making from $400,000 to $800,000 per year smuggling. I entered into a fight against them, confiscated over $324,000 of their property and put 26 of these men in the jail. They then went for me, and the Democratic administration generally, and even bought or controlled the Democratic papers and made them attack nearly all of Mr. Cleveland's appointees.

I am now as you can see practicing law here. I opened this office when I quit the Federal office but during my labors among the shipping I contracted so many colds that it resulted in a catarrh in the head, which is so severe on me that I fear that I will have to change to a milder climate. I often hear from Gus through Jones Brothers and Dr. Bell. Am pleased to know that you are getting along as happily as the best majority of mankind, and pray for your continuance.

Most of our old Trinity friends have gone to the "other side." John Martin, Jess Bennett, Joe Sturdevant, John Carter, Rodger Bates, B. M. George, W. S. Louden, and a few others are only left. The county is developing some rich quartz mines near Lewiston, North Fork, New River, and Canon Creek.

Your son promised when I met him to call at this office, but so far has not come around. I presume he will come with the Captain when the holidays are over, when I will be pleased to do what I can for him.

Truly your friend,

Wiley J. Tinnin

Tom Is In Town

May 24, 1891

Dear Brother.

It is Sunday, and I am resting at home, which I have done damned nearly all the Sundays this year. I have neglected to write you. I have not forgotten you for you are ever in my thoughts. But you must not delay in writing me. I suppose Tom has told you about my work. He has not been very generous in letting me know his whereabouts. He was at my place this spring and did some work for me. He made me a map for the Park. I was so busy and could not give him any help or very little attention. He is in the railroad company employ at Fresno, California – at a pretty good salary, too, so William Bell informs me. The job was probably arranged by Wiley Tinnin, but apparently Tom did not stay with it for long.

I have been hard at work all this year preparing to put the Park property in shape for sale. This is a big job and an expensive one. It will take me all this year and I hope to live through it. I have been on the grounds every morning, rain or shine, before seven o'clock when the men go to work. Pretty heavy for an old man. I have moved and rebuilt about seven dwellings and am nearly complete. I started in without one dollar. Have expended up to this time about $5,000 and it will require about the same amount to complete. This would not be bad but I was in debt at the start. I intend to have a big auction. The property will sell quickly when I get it in shape. I will only sell lots. The houses being mine and Jennie's income. So I have all I want to look after but, I think I am equal for the emergency.

I get very tired during the day, but thank God I am all right. All is done by the day workers - carpenters, brick masons, plasterers. Plumbers are the worst of the lot. I buy all materials. It was a big job for me, but I had to do something. The property was running behind with the property taxes and street improvements. It will come out all right. This had to be done, and I can do it.

I hope this will find you all well. We are tolerably well.

Jennie sends her love to you and yours.

Your affectionate brother,

Thomas W. Badger

Tom Explores California

San Francisco, California

July 26, 1891

My Dear Father:

Your postal rec'd some time ago. I should have answered sooner but have had nothing in particular to write about. The RR company has stopped work and I am taking a rest for a while. I do not know exactly how long it will be before I am put to work again. I have been nearly all over the state and I think I have a pretty fair knowledge of California from one end to the other. It is a great country and I think you and Cousin Joe made a great mistake when you left it (when he returned to Red Bank). *If you had taken up land in the right places you might be worth your millions now. What do you think of farming land selling for $1,000 per acre? What do you think of a 12-acre orchard that produces a crop that sells for $3,000?*

If a man has money enough to start in most any line he can make money out here, but it is about as slow out here for the man who has to work for his daily wages as it is back east. There are fifty tramps in California for every one in Virginia and you find men at that business of all trades and professions. They call them "Howbows" (hobos) *out here. They still make California stew. I suppose it is the same kind I have heard you and Cousin Joe talk about.*

I don't know but what I would have done just as well or better if I had remained in the East. This country is over-stocked with engineers and surveyors, and although there are probably just as many in the east they have much more work than we do out here. You see there is but one RR in the whole state and when it stops work you are out of work.

I suppose John LeCato and wife (Lavinia) *are back by this time. Give my kindest regards to all friends and tell them that I am still alive. Let me hear from you when you can.*

Your son,

T.N. Badger

Tom apparently had a falling-out with his aunt and uncle, as he implies in the following letter. It appears that Capt. Tom might have arranged a position for Tom that Tom felt was below his expectations. And Tom also expresses some envy of his uncle's business dealings.

Loafing Is Hard Work

2435 California St.

San Francisco, July 4ᵗʰ 1892

My dear Father,

Your kind letter received. No, I am not into anything that will pay me better yet. The prospect is fair at this time for me to loaf for the next two months.

I have been offered a position that will pay me $60 + all expenses (equal to about $90) but it is not available until Sept 1ˢᵗ. I expect it is better than anything I could do at home. I have been here now nearly a month and I find this loafing hard work indeed. I may go out on a camping expedition next week. In the meantime, my pocketbook is growing lighter every day. I know beyond a doubt that I would have been better off had I not known a <u>soul</u> in this infernal country, for then I would have been free to do as I pleased. To have accepted what ever came along. But now I know everybody, that is to say they know me. (better than I do myself).

I never go on the street but what I see people by the score that I have met in the various positions I have held. So you see I can't go out and work for my living like a stranger. If I do I sacrifice all chances for something better.

I have some friends here who are staunch and sound as long as my money lasts. My friends in need I can count without the use of my fingers or toes either.

I am standing on my own bottom out here. Every position I have filled so far has been obtained by my own efforts and had I have depended on my friends I would have long since died of starvation. I have nothing to say against them. The money they have is theirs and they are welcome to keep it. An Eastern Shore man and a Californian are as different as Dr. Jekyl and Mr. Hyde.

Uncle Tom is selling away and handling his thousands. He owns some six or eight blocks of property valued from $5,000 to $500 per lot. I have been told by reliable parties that he was offered $115,000 last year for the park alone. I enclose you a map that I made of part of his property. If you were to see him again you will find him a very different man from what he was when you knew him. His wife is the arch-fiend personified and they fight and scratch like dogs and cats. They are about the most miserable couple I know of.

Uncle Tom says he has not received any letters from Aunt Lavinia and hence of course is excusable for not answering. I am glad to hear that John has improved. His improvement is certainly miraculous. Give my love to all friends and tell them I hope to see them in1893.

Your son,

T. N. Badger

P.S.: Please burn all my letters

John W. Badger, back at home on the farm in Red Bank, is worried about his son in California. Thomas advises him not to worry, saying that his experiences in California are all part of his education. He lends Tom some money to travel to a job in Winton.

TOM HAS JOB TROUBLE

February 27, 1893

Dear Brother,

Yours of 18th January is at hand and contents noted. I think you need not be distressed about Tom. It is true that I have no children, nor do I have any desire for them. Old age has not numbed my sensibilities or affected my mental abilities. My mind is as clear at this time as it ever has been.

I think you are a little sensitive about Tom. All the experience he has obtained in California is part of his education. He is about old enough to take care of his self, and there are lots of people here that have to do the same. The trouble is he never felt he had to rely on his own resources. If he had known that he could not obtain money from other sources, and had to depend on his own energy, he would have acted different. He would have kept his place of employment and tried to please his employer. Now he will not stay in any situation. Tom does not appear to think for tomorrow. The Bells have done all they can for him. I have been willing to do, but I have no political influence and do not mix much with people. I never go out at night on account of my health. I had not given Tom any money until last Saturday the 25th. I sent him ten dollars. He is welcome.

I saw Tom about ten days ago at my little affair. He then told me that he had failed to secure the place that he had previously told me he could get, and wanted to know what was the best thing for him to do. I talked with him, and I thought gave him sound advice. He did not ask me then for money, and I did not offer him any at that time. I told him to go to work at anything he could find. He wrote me that he had received employment in Winton (a small town on the Santa Fe Railroad line), *but had not the money to get out of town. I lent him the amount. He wants to go soon.*

Why I have not written is not that I do not think of you, but simply that I have nothing pleasant to write about. I have been waiting, thinking something might turn up so that I could send you a little money, but all luck disappeared.

I am at work. I cannot afford to have skilled men to work. It costs too much; consequently I am tied down at home. Jennie has been wanting to go off on a trip. I have had no money to give her. She has sold 2 cows, also furniture from the house. She has been very faithful. I have used her money to kick along. There is little or nothing in real estate. Everybody is hard up.

We are in pretty good health. Hope you and yours are as well. Jennie sends you a kiss.

Thomas W. Badger

THE BANKS ARE FAILING

Oakland, July 18th 1893

John W. Badger

Northampton Co, Va.

It has been some time since I wrote you. It is not because I do not think of you. You and other friends are my daily thought. I have been in hopes that I would have a little let up in my old age. I now almost despair. I did pretty well until about 3 months ago. Sold property real estate in the amount of about $15,000. Paid up mortgages to the amount of $10,000 which was not doing much. I should have sold $20,000 worth but I was satisfied if I could have continued on as I had been doing. Another year like the last would place me in a comfortable condition.

Everything is to a stand still though has only been a few bank failures here and do not think any (more) will fail. Plenty of money in the bank, but will not give it out. Even the depositors cannot draw their money, only under 60 days worth. So there is a complete stagnation in all kinds of business. I owe a large amount yet. I only owe the bank and they are secured by mortgage.

I have house half complete but will not go in until things are settled. I was in hopes I would be able to dispose of property to square off my indebtedness before my demise, but it is … I am now in a few years 66 years old. I have felt older this year. I am trouble with the rheumatism. They are all getting worse. I take no medicine.

I am anxious to straighten out my affairs so I can make deed to your property. It is uppermost in my mind to arrange matter and our working to that end. You will be fine…..Keep this to yourself,

Love to all,

Your Brother T. W. Badger

Since leaving VMI, Tom taught school, worked as an engineer for the Coast Survey in Washington, joined the engineering staff of Pennsylvania Railroad, and then moved to California to work for a railroad company in Fresno. In the few years since leaving college, Tom did not exactly put together a glowing resume of work history. He appears to have become estranged from his aunt and uncle, probably because he did not follow up on jobs his uncle arranged for him. He saw little of his aunt and uncle between 1893 and 1899, and in one letter he says the Captain had discouraged him from visiting.

But Tom seems to have hit his stride during this period. Tom went back to school and earned a degree in mechanical engineering from the University of California at Berkeley in 1899. He then went into business for himself and the letterheads in his correspondence list numerous projects and specialties he was involved with. After a shaky start, Tom seems to have found his path. He was much more comfortable being self-employed than being a salaried employee. His energy, initiative, and creativity eventually made him a success.

Unfortunately, the Captain and Jennie would not live to witness his good fortune. In June 1899 Tom wrote to his father with news that his aunt and uncle were in failing health. Jennie had fallen and had suffered a heart attack. The Captain was dealing possibly with Alzheimer's as well as physical issues.

Emeryville, California, June 16, 1899

My Dear Father:

Your letter rec'd some time ago now. I have been very busy and should have answered sooner. I delivered your letter to Uncle Tom and he appeared glad to hear from you. He told me to write and give his love and said that he would write but that he had a great deal of trouble with his head since his sickness, in fact, he said that he came very near losing his mind and that his head has not been so that he could do anything since. He said he would try to write before long.

I saw him again today downtown where I am at work. He is very little better he says and has very little hope of getting well. Said he would try to write you in a few days. I had quite a talk with him. He appears to be rational enough all right. Said he was done with the Bells from now on, also that Josie had been over to see his wife several times, notwithstanding the fact that he had ordered her out of his house. His wife has been quite sick, fell on the sidewalk, and was unconscious for some time with heart trouble. Let me hear from you. I must close now. Your devoted son,

Thos. N. Badger

The Captain Nears the End

Emeryville, California, November 1, 1899

Dear Father:

Your interesting letter received now some two months ago. I have been so busy that I have had no time to write. I am running two jobs and they keep me on the go all the time. Last week Uncle Tom sent for me to come see him and I went. The first time I had been in his house for about six years. Once when I was down in the world, he told me it would be best for me not to come, so I have followed his advice.

It was about the saddest mission of my life. He does not expect to live but a few weeks or months at most. It was a sad picture and one that I will never forget. His wife met me and informed me he was at home and went and told him I was there. He invited me in and I talked about two hours with him, about you and home and himself. I wanted him to go home (to Virginia) but he said it was too late now. He was so much affected he could hardly talk to me. Said he would like to be buried back there with the rest, but it did not matter much.

He said he had been trying to write you for some time but that he had been unable to finish his letters on account of his head. Write to him at once. He wants to hear from you. He did not say anything in particular about his business affairs, and I do not care to broach the subject with him unless you want me to.

The old man is not now, nor has he been for some time, more than a child. Write me what you want before it is too late. He thanked me for coming to see him and I promised to come see him as often as I could. I offered to let him have what money I had, but he said they had gotten all they needed from a friend.

I have never had anything in my life make me feel so badly as that visit to him did. He suffers a great deal and cannot sleep, seems to think he is losing his mind. He said his wife has done everything for him that she can do. She is not much better off.

If you want him to come home I can come with him. I am about through my work at the race track and expect to be in Emeryville next week. Telegraph me if you want the money to come out here. I have about $500 on hand at your disposal. Hope you are well and comfortably fixed for the winter. Write me at once.

Your devoted son,

Thos. N. Badger

Within three weeks of Thomas's visit, the Captain was dead. He did not get to return to Virginia, nor did his brother get to visit him one final time. The *San Francisco Chronicle* did a story on him shortly before he died:

> "The captain is one of the best known pioneers of the city, and indeed at one time owned a large portion of the territory on which Oakland is built. He is an old sailor-pioneer, having followed a life at sea until he landed in San Francisco on the 5th of August, 1849. For a long while he engaged in the shipping business in San Francisco, and had vessels trading all over the coast."

Within three months, Jennie also was dead. Captain Tom and Jennie were buried in Laurel Hill Cemetery alongside Charles Falkenburg. Their grave was marked by the sculpted likeness of the bark *Jane A. Falkenburg*.

A full obituary for Thomas Badger is in Appendix C. Also see the chapter "And Now a Third Generation of Thomas Badgers..." for information on Laurel Hill Cemetery and the Pioneers buried there.

A New Century, A New Era

The new century ushered in a new era for the Badger family in California. The Captain and First Lady died within weeks of each other, and Thomas became a lifetime Californian. He married Emily Burns, who grew up in Alabama, and the couple built a two-story house on Linden Avenue in Berkely. Thomas remained a prolific letter writer, and he freely dispensed advice on everything from health and fitness to financial investments. He wrote letters mainly to his father, until his father died in 1905, and then to his brother Tank, and now and then to a nephew on special occasions.

Uncle Tom, as he was known to my generation of the family, was a bit of a mystery relative. He existed in family lore, but few had ever met him. If he and Emily visited the family on the Eastern Shore of Virginia, the occasion was not documented. He often described his wife as being sickly, but then in a letter he would report on a five-mile mountain hike the two took together. In one letter, he said that a trip back east would be too much for her. In fact, he says little about her, other than she enjoyed gardening at their Linden Avenue home. In his letters, he refers to her as "my wife," seldom if ever using her given name.

Thomas N. Badger's letterhead from 1905

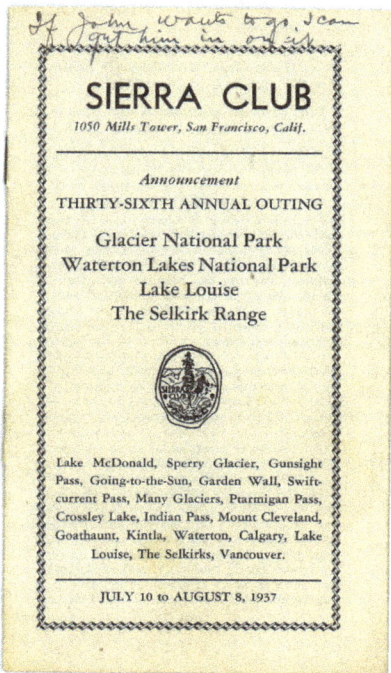

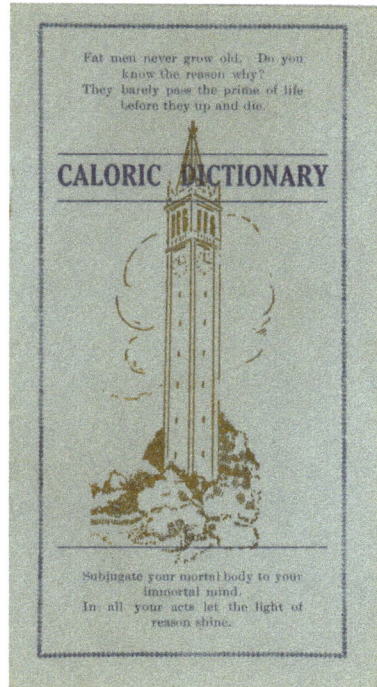

Thomas N. was an avid hiker and a charter member of the Sierra Club. The brochure promotes the 36th annual outing, a hike in Glacier National Park. He also wrote a Caloric Dictionary long before the general public became concerned with calories.

Eccentric could be an accurate adjective to describe Uncle Tom. He worked as an engineer, and was apparently good at it. He laid out sections of the community of Emeryville, a community north of Oakland on San Francisco Bay, and he was often paid in building lots. A large portion of his income apparently came from the rental of houses. He was an avid hiker and fitness buff, and though he lived to be nearly ninety, he thought he was near death from about age sixty on.

Uncle Tom was also an amateur inventor, putting those engineering skills to the test. He designed a disappearing stairway, disappearing mailbox, and a box-bottom bag. He wrote a brochure on the caloric table long before the general public began concerning themselves with calories. He was an avid hiker, an original member of the Sierra Hiking Club, and he remained physically active for most of his life, although he complained regularly about his health.

Hal Johnson wrote a column in the *Berkeley Gazette* titled "So We're Told," and on October 24, 1939 he did this profile of Tom Badger:

OLDEST BOY SCOUT

"On almost any day you are downtown you are likely to run into a khaki-clad man with a walking stick. Nobody would guess that he had turned 70, for this oldest Boy Scout steps along with a military stride not for blocks but for miles.

He is Thomas Badger of 2946 Linden Street, a native of Virginia who almost would rather walk than eat. Every day in the year, regardless of weather, he averages ten miles of walking, and then for special recreation he does a little climbing. He has hiked almost every trail in California as a member of the Sierra Club.

Did you ever hear of Mt. Badger? It is up in the Berkeley Hills at the end of Claremont Ridge. The Berkeley Hiking Club named it for Badger because he is one of the few persons who ever was able to scale it before he built a good trail up this almost vertical ledge. Until Badger cut in the footholds, only Alpine guides would have thought of attempting the 150-foot straight up climb.

Years ago when Badger followed the profession of civil engineering he was the city engineer of Emeryville and Benicia. He laid out Mountain View Cemetery. When he found that local hikers were trying to scale what is now Mt. Badger he thought he had better cut some steps to prevent Mountain View from being over populated with amateur mountain climbers."

We have letters from Uncle Tom to his brother Tank right up to the time of Tank's death. When he could no longer write, a friend and fellow Mason wrote them for him, describing his final months in a nursing home in Berkley. He died on January 24, 1954 and members of the family from my generation never met him. But through these letters, we follow him from the time he entered VMI at age 16 until he died in California and was buried there. We never knew him, yet in a way we became very familiar with him. We read his words, and we can hear him speak.

The next series of letters are from Tom to his father back home at Red Bank.

THINGS ARE LOOKING UP

Thomas N. Badger

Civil Engineer, Surveyor and Draughtsman

426 Orange Street

Oakland, CA

Sept. 15, 1901

My dear Father,

Your welcome letter to hand. I have been so busy that this is the first opportunity I have had to answer. Things have been coming my way for once at least in a financial way. I have collected about $700 since July 1. So you see it would not do for me to get out of line now. I think in about two weeks I will be through my Emeryville job where about $700 more will be due me. I will come home just so soon as I can sometime between now and Xmas if the Good Lord is willing that I should. I hope you are in better health than when you last wrote.

No prospect of settling the estate any time soon. (The estate of Thomas W. Badger)

Wright the administrator informed me that it would possibly be 5 years before he settled it. Nobody bothers him but myself. I told him he had to settle it at once or I would know the reason why he did not do so.

I want to get a few thousand dollars together so that I may not be quite so helpless as I have been in the past.

Your devoted son,

Thos. N. Badger

Enclosure P. O. Order $10.00

Tell Aunt Lavinia to write to Wright and demand that he settle the estate at once.

Burn This Letter

Thomas N. Badger

July 11, 1902

Dear Father,

Your letter received. Glad to hear from you and that you are so much better than you were. I hope you may continue to improve. The property that I referred to was sold by Wright for $600. I understand it was in my uncle's name. I will do what I can to get it. I have written Tank to buy the Robins place. Don't say anything about it to any one except Tank. Burn this letter as soon as you read it. Tell Tank to buy it as soon as possible.

Have not heard from Cousin Joe, maybe he won't write to me as I took such an old looking picture of him and said it was good. I expect to go to work next week on a $50,000 job. Send me receipt for the Century that I sent you. What do you think of this oyster business? Write when you can.

Your son,

Thos. N. Badger

Father Faces Surgery

May 10, 1903

My dear Father,

Your long and interesting letter received and I assure you appreciated. I have read it over several times. It made me feel faint when I first read it, but I feel better now. It is a source of regret to me that I have not been able to see more of you and to be with you. It is no small matter to be 3,000 miles away from all of your blood relations. I don't believe I would ever want to see the old place again after you are gone. It is barely possible that I may come home this summer. I have no big jobs on hand and could come for two months without losing much. I would come possibly in July. It may be I will be busy by that time and unable to come but <u>I intend to come if I can.</u> Money doesn't amount to much in this world. The love of you and noble character is a great deal more to me.

Now about the operation. I want to tell you that surgery has made wonderful strides in the past 20 years. They do wonderful things now. I know of many older than you who have recently been successfully operated on for cancer of the hip. I know another who had his stomach removed and is well and hearty today. He is about 60.

Personally, I would take chances with the operation if it were the only health restorer. Life is not much at its best, and when we have to endure continual suffering, it would be almost unbearable to me. But you know better than anyone else whether you could stand it or not. A certain amount of vitality is <u>absolutely necessary.</u> Nature must be strong enough to heal the wounds, otherwise it would be folly to make them. What does your doctor advise you? If you go, you should remain until you have completely recovered which would take about six weeks. I know of no reason why the Badgers should die at 70 and other families live to be 80, 90 or 100. You have led a temperate life except that you have <u>worried too much.</u> That kills people quicker than disease of the body. You are like myself, inclined to be pessimistic which does not promote longevity.

So, father, you alone can decide what is best to do. I can furnish you $500 any time you say you want it. Come out to see me, and see again the glorious mountains where you spent your youth and breathe once more the fragrance of their pines and drink once more of their pure waters. I know you are often here in your dreams. Well Father I will do whatever I conscientiously can for, not only, Susie and Maggie but for every other member of your family.

Well father I must close. Bear up, be cheerful, you may bury a whole lot of us yet. I hope when this reaches you you may be much improved and that you may have many years yet to stay with us.

Write to me when you are able.

Your devoted son,

Thos. N. Badger

A Trip To Mendocino

June 14, 1903

Dear Father,

Today is Sunday, windy, damp and gloomy so thought I would stay in and write. I believe I did not write you about my trip to Mendocino Co. to see the stock ranch that I wrote you about. The railroad runs up the Russian River Valley most of the way. It is the most beautiful country I have ever seen. Vineyards and orchards as far as you can see, delightful climate, no fog, dry. They tell me they get $100 per acre for the grapes on the vine. Olives and nuts are equally profitable.

Well, I did not buy the ranch. I found out that it had been offered once for $1,600. They asked me $5,000. It is a beautiful place, lots of magnificent trees on it but very little of it could be cultivated. In fact, there was too much hard work in sight to suit me. I would like to own 100 acres of level land in the valley where a man can get greater returns for his efforts. City life doesn't suit me. I don't get exercise sufficient to keep in good health. My eyes are beginning to play out on me from reading and drafting. I would much prefer to have constant employment at outdoor work. I'm not doing much now in the way of money-making earn about $100 a month. I'm afraid the oyster business is a failure, as I knew it would be unless someone was on the ground continually. Tank talks of planting in the creek. He can't hold them there any better than at Prouts Island in my opinion.

In fact, to make a success of oysters as with everything else "one must give his whole time and attention and camp on the ground." I don't know what Tank makes out of the store but if he makes a living he is taking chances when he gives it up. My work is very uncertain. I may get out and not yet able to find employment for months or even years. So it certainly behooves me to try to hold on to what I have saved. The $500 I have in the hardware business *has earned at the rate of 11% for the first six months, so I think that's all OK.*

I don't care to invest any more money now on my place at home in perishable improvements. I will put a good wire fence around the lot Shields wants, but that's as far as I care to go. I believe you know Shields to be OK as a neighbor. If you have any doubt about him, don't let him have the lot. My principal object in buying that place was to rid you of disagreeable people and I want to keep you rid of them from now on, so consider well before he builds. I think if he located around by Onancock there would be much less chance of friction in the future. Now I leave the whole matter with you to do with as you would your own property

I sent you a magazine called "Sunset" for a year beginning with the June number. Please let me know if it arrives and how you like it. Well, I must close. I hope you are well and happy. Write when you can.

Give my love to all.

Your son,

Thos. N. Badger

The magazine *Sunset* Tom was referring to is still being published today. It was originally published by Southern Pacific Railroad in San Francisco to encourage people to visit California. The "June number" included a story by a young writer from San Francisco named Jack London titled "The Faith of Man." The magazine is a collectors' item today.

Working On The Railroad

July 21, 1903

Dear Father,

I intended to write to you about two weeks ago but business struck me and I have been on the jump ever since. Have a job now with the Santa Fe Railroad that I think will last until Xmas. It has been over ten years since I did any R.R. work so I had to work hard, and several other things came at the same time and I am just beginning to get my breath.

81

I received your letter and was much relieved, also two or three from Tank since. I hope your health may continue to improve. Give Aunt Lavinia my congratulations. I understand Uncle Able is worth $20,000. I sent Maggie a standard cook book. The information it contains is of more practical value to a young lady than any other half dozen books that I know of, what do you think of it? I hope they don't make you sick with some of the fancy dishes. The book I think as a whole contains lots of practical every day information. Let me know when you want to send Maggie to school. I believe she is about 14 now, is she not, and I presume this year or next you will want to send her to Onancock or some similar school. So let me know just what you and she want to do. It is too bad Willie cannot have a year in school. I think George might easily take his place from November 1st to February 1st this year. That will give him 4 months. He can do a lot in that time. He might keep it up for two for three years. Tell him to write me if he wants to do it, and if the arrangement can be made and what the cost will be.

I haven't any great amount of ready money, but I want to do some good if I can with what I have. Money is a delusion and a snare unless good use is made of it. I believe I spent between $150 and $200 the year I spent at Onancock. You tell Willie and the girls to communicate with me whenever they have a plan decided on. Tell them to ascertain what the expenses will be and I will see if I can't do the rest.

I will make I think about $2,000 this year, and so far as money goes I suppose I may consider myself fairly well fixed and then my experience will enable me to command a good position anywhere.

I expect to come home next year on a pass without fail.

Write when you can. I have been trying to get the N.Y. address of the California Wine Association so that I can order wine for you from there. Let me know when you want anything.

Your devoted son,

Thos N. Badger

May 15, 1904

My dear Father,

I had a letter from Tank yesterday telling me of your sickness and suffering. I wish I could be with you, for possibly I might be able to help to alleviate your suffering in some way. Don't give up and say it's no use. It's a duty to do what we can to keep our bodies in working order, until time has relieved us of the duty, and to use the language of Oliver Wendell Holmes – "When wasting ago and wearying strife have sapped the leaning walls of life, Oh Father grant thy love divine to make these mystic temples thine."

I don't think the Creator intended that we should suffer bodily pains for long. Most all our suffering could be avoided if we would use all the means at our command in order to be relieved. Now then if you can think of anything that you think will possibly relieve you in any way, it will be my <u>greatest pleasure to provide it for you.</u> I can get 3 or 4 thousand dollars any day I want it, so don't think for once that I am financially embarrassed. I expect to pay off all that I owe by next fall and possibly will have sold all my property by that time. I want to put about $5,000 on a good farm there at home and it will be a place I can go to and live when necessity requires it. My eyes will not permit me to do much more office work, and it is the dream of my life to get back on the farm and do appetizing, health-giving outdoor work, not 14 hours a day as you have done but about for 7.

Tomorrow is a big day in Berkeley and Emeryville. The Santa Fe has completed its transcontinental line and its main depot is in Emeryville. I am going to take some pictures of the celebration to send you. Prospects are good here now for this year. I enclose $20, also a little book of specifications that I have just gotten out, expect to do about $100,000 worth of work under them. With love to you and all my friends on the E.S.

Your devoted son,

Thos. N. Badger

June 15, 1904

My dear Father,

Your long and interesting letter received and read with much pleasure. I am glad to know your health is improved. I can't see why you should be troubled about the girls. They are both nearly grown and have a large circle of relatives all of whom will be more than glad to help them. I think you have a great deal to be thankful for. Contrast your position with that of Uncle Tom's. His last days were spent in bitter disappointment, harassed by his load of debt and his wife anxious to be rid of him for mercenary reasons. I have always been glad that you have a home in the country where you can walk about and occupy your mind and time.

I will do what I can for the girls. If I succeed in converting my property into money this year I will give them outright what you think they need. I am afraid the presidential election is going to put a damper on business of all kind, so all I can say is that you may count on me to do the right thing when I am in a position to. You understand I owe some money, and you know what that means. Once you let the interest get started on you then your name is "mud." It would be suicidal for me to quit here now and go to spending money. Uncle Tom borrowed $2,000 to go home with and he carried the load to his grave. If I can make a sale and clean up my debts you will see me home in a short time. Tell the girls to learn how to do useful things. The ornamental predominated in the Southern Educational Institutions. Thirty years from now will show great changes in the South. I was startled to read in the paper I got from home that the negroes actually own three-quarters of the land in Northampton County, and it is my prediction that 30 years from now they will own three-quarters of it. They do the work, the useful things. The working people get the land and the fullness thereof in all free countries. If I were living at home I would supply myself with all modern mechanical labor-saving appliances and do my own work of all kind. You can get a windmill now that will pump your water, saw your wood, shell corn, wash your clothes, grind your meal and do a thousand and one other things.

If the white people of the south don't make a change they are doomed to be driven out of the country, so I say by all means teach your children the useful things of life. I am indeed sorry Willie cannot have a chance to improve his mind, for I think there is more promise in him than any or all the rest of us – and why? The answer is he is naturally as intelligent, or I think I can safely say more intelligent by nature than the rest of us, and he is a "WORKER." You know none of the rest of us are except Tank, and he did not care for books. The Worker will land on top every time if his labor is intelligently applied.

I will send you some more wine. I will be home as soon as I can. Don't worry about anything, in fact, I can't see that you have anything to worry about as long as you can keep out of pain and be as comfortable as possible. The future I know is troubling you, for the unselfish life you have led can leave you no doubts in that direction. I cannot recall one single act of yours that would disturb the peace of mind of the most sensitive conscience. May your children one and all strive to emulate the good example you have given us.

Write as often as you feel able to do so.

Your devoted son,

Thos N. Badger

MAKING BREAD AND WASHING CLOTHES

July 31, 1904

My dear Father,

Your long and interesting letter received and appreciated. Have been waiting, hoping that I might have something worth writing about. All my big jobs for this summer have gone a glimmering so far, but suppose I must not complain as I earn something over $100 every month. My investments are very promising at the present time but I have made no sales since I wrote you. I am quite certain I will have lots of money in a few years but wish I had more now. I suppose I will have to build a house for Goffigon, and that will take about all I can put together. I hope your health is good and that your wants are supplied.

Now as to Maggie I suggest that she get the books for the first half of the school term and do the work at home. I know she can do it if she only thinks so. If she will do this I will try to furnish the money for the last half of the term. When will you want to send Susie? Tell Maggie and Susie that I want them to send me a certificate from you showing that they are competent to make wheat bread, corn bread, in fact to cook a good square meal, to milk, and to do _their own_ washing. I don't mean this for a joke but am in dead earnest about it.

I hope Tank is not sick. I don't think he places as much value on my advice as he might do profitably. I told him the city people would have no money this summer. If ever I come back to the E. S. to live I shall try to raise something that always pays a small profit such as chickens, hogs, cattle, horses, ducks, etc. It would not make me happy to know that I was working hard only to feed the Yanks. The weather here is very pleasant, in fact all over California. I hope I may get back home next summer, be out of debt and have some money.

Give my love to all. Your devoted son,

Thos N. Badger

MAGGIE GOES TO SCHOOL

October 2, 1904

Dear Father,

I received your letter of August 29 and I believe have written you once before since then. Perhaps I over estimated in thinking Maggie could do the half-years work at home. I have known a number of students to do it but they were doing more advanced work and their minds were more mature. If she could pass the examination, certainly the directors would allow her to take her place in the class. If they would not I certainly have no faith in their integrity. All the colleges give a student full credit for all he knows no matter where or how he acquired the knowledge. After thinking the matter over, I don't know that Maggie could accomplish the work unaided, and as a little learning is a dangerous thing, she had better return with her class and continue her work.

I enclose you a draft on New York for Two Hundred Dollars ($200.) If

86

that is not enough to cover her expenses for the year I will send all she needs. Tell Maggie to buy everything she really needs - clothes and everything else. I don't want her to feel she has to stint herself in the least. I have been along that road and can appreciate her position. I have only one request to make of her and it is that she keep an itemized account of her expenditures and send it to me complete at the end of the school year. I ask her to do this in order that she may learn how to keep track of money. No Southern woman I have ever known had acquired sufficient knowledge of accounts to do it. She wrote me last year that she had not spent any money that she did not have to, which I know was true, but this bookkeeping is a fad of mine and I hope she will comply with my request.

Give my love to everybody. Had a long letter from Tank. He thinks Maggie should go on to school. Am happy that I can make it possible for her to do so.

Your son, Thos N Badger

TOM BIDS FAREWELL TO HIS FATHER

John Wesley Badger died on August 1, 1905, so he never got to read the final letter sent from California by his son Tom. Tank had sent Tom a telegram on July 28 informing him that their father's condition was grave. Tom replied by telegram, and then composed this final letter to his father that he realized would probably never be read.

July 30, 1905

My Dear Father,

Two days ago I received from Tank a telegram announcing your extreme illness. I answered and you no doubt have received my telegram. I am afraid this letter will not reach you, for I know as well as you do the end is near, also the beginning of life eternal is at hand. To me the thought of leaving this pain-racked, perishable body, to return to mother earth from whence we came, is an inspiration, a hope we can all look forward to with <u>certainty</u>. We know that pain, suffering, earthly disappointments, in fact, all the earthly troubles of this clay house of ours terminate forever and instantly when dissolution comes to our relief. Beyond dissolution of the body, by which the spirit of man is set from, we certainly can have only hope. We all know that every human being has an individuality distinct and not made of clay and not perishable as the body. We see here on earth that while we are all from the same earth and originated in the same manner, and should be in all respects alike, and yet – how different we are. Certainly our bodies are alike perishable, and subject to all the shortcoming that flesh is heir to. But the immortal, the mind, the noble character stands out clear and distinct as only a tenant of the earthly body. _Knowing_ as we all do that God is and always has been, that He created us subject to His laws, which are the laws of Nature.

How can we feel other than thankful when our earthly task is ended and we are called to the great beyond, knowing that we are obeying one of the laws of our Creator? Can anyone doubt the kind Providence that has been with us in this world? I know you have no doubts on this subject. No human being ever departed this world without some regrets for his past life. God made us only human. Had all our acts and thoughts been just what we would like to have had them when we think over them at the end, we would have been Divinities and not men. I remember once when I was about 6 years old someone suggested to me that you were going to die. I can distinctly remember the agony of mind that came over me, in fact it was overwhelming. I feel the same way today to a certain extent. The only difference is I can now look beyond the parting. I know that it is but a _day_ when we will _all_ pass to the far side, and to the inheritance prepared for us by the giver of all good and perfect gifts. Let us part for this day with the hopes that a grand reunion awaits us, and a firm trust in God our Creator and the Creator of the Heavens and the Earth. When I last saw you I hoped to be home again before now to stay but my hopes have not been realized. I thought it best for me to remain here. That I could accomplish more good by staying. I would start for home immediately if I followed my inclination but I am just now in the midst of a big job of work which I should have to abandon. I am with you in spirit if not in body.

Any request you have to make of me will be most faithfully performed. Tell Tank all you would have said to me were I there.

Your devoted son,

Thos N Badger

Intermission

There is a gap of nearly 25 years between Tom's farewell letter to his father and a subsequent series of letters to his brother, Tank. What happened to the letters is anyone's guess. Perhaps they were simply not saved, or were discarded during an overly enthusiastic spring cleaning. Or, they might still be in an old cardboard box stashed in an attic or closet somewhere.

The two brothers clearly changed during that hiatus. Tom had lived in California for nearly 40 years at that point, he had married, and at age 62 had lost the enthusiasm and optimism of his younger days. His letters became brief and sometimes bitter. He writes of not being able to find work, of deadbeat tenants, of physical issues, and although he lived to be almost 90, he seemed to feel in his sixties that the end was near.

Things had changed for Tank also. He bought a farm in the village of Birds Nest, so named for a nearby tavern, and he farmed about 60 acres, worked on the water, operated a store for some time, and had a barrel-making business in the village. The railroad came to the Eastern Shore in 1884, and commerce gradually moved from the boat landings to the railroad stations. Tank bought his farm in 1905, built a large frame two-story farm house, barns, a corn crib, smokehouse, henhouse, and various other accoutrements necessary for a working farm. Tank could stand on his front porch and see the steam-powered locomotives go by a short distance east of his farm.

The Great Depression obviously had an effect on both men. Tom's income was mainly from rental property, and tenants were difficult to come by because jobs were scarce. His letters express his growing frustration with government, the economy, and an increasingly chaotic society. Tank also had little income, but he was a farmer and his family raised most of their own food.

Both brothers got married in 1901, Tom to Emily Burns and Tank to Maggie Sarah Hallett, who was from Capeville, a few miles south of Birds Nest. Little is known about Emily. The Badger-Tankard book describes her as being from the "deep south," but little else is offered, and she is not often mentioned in family correspondence. Tom sometimes mentions her in letters, but rarely in affectionate terms. In most of the letters, he refers to her simply as "my wife," seldom using her given name.

Maggie did this charcoal sketch of Jennie, her younger sister.

Maggie, on the other hand, was a local girl well known to the family. She was a devoted farmer's wife, taught Sunday school at Johnson's Church for many years, and could churn butter, make scrapple and souse, and bake a mean poundcake. She also was a talented artist, although only two of her charcoal sketches are known to exist. Our family has a portrait of Jennie, Maggie's younger sister, and there is also a self-portrait that belongs to a cousin. These are drawings by a gifted person, and she must have done many more in her lifetime. It's a shame they are gone.

Tom and Emily had no children, but Tank and Miss Mag had five: Mary Frances, Thomas Hallett (my father), Norman, John Tankard, Jr., and Curtis Lamar. Lamar, the youngest, took over the family farm after Tank's death in 1953. The other men also had farm-related careers. John taught agriculture at Northampton High School, Hallett worked for the Eastern Shore of Virginia Produce Exchange, and Norman had a farm of his own a short distance from the home place.

The Badger brothers, sons of Tank and Maggie Badger: from left, Hallett, Norman, Lamar, and John, Jr. An older sister, Mary Frances, died before this photograph was taken.

RED BANK LANDING

Thomas N. Badger

P. O. Box 126

Berkeley, Calif.

Phone Berkeley 1925-J, 5 to 7 A.M. or P.M.

To: Mr. J. T. Badger

Birds Nest, Northampton Co., Virginia

October 21, 1929

Dear Brother,

 Your letter received and many thanks for your offer of the old place (Red Bank Landing). *My wife would be unable to travel that far. Two hours in an automobile does her up completely. I have gotten strong with the doctor treatments and am feeling much better now. They were so severe that they put me out. I do not think I will ever be the same again. Am too old to come back completely. Seven or eight years more and I will be 70. Quitting time for most of us.*

Yesterday I went down to my 40 acres in the Santa Cruz Mountains. It was great down there. I have redwood trees large enough to build several houses. 2,000 feet above sea level. Very dry now. I am sending you a goose-duck book. One of my friends has an Indian Runner that lays 350 eggs a year. The old place would be fine for 1,000 ducks. They would produce at least $5,000 a year net.

How is your wife?

Your brother,

Thos N. Badger

Bad Times in Berkeley

Thomas N. Badger

2946 Linden Avenue

Berkeley, Calif.

July 17, 1934

Dear Brother,

Your letter and John's picture received. John is a fine promising boy. I certainly wish I could help your boys to get a start in life. I am not able anymore to satisfy my own wants. The whole country is in desperate straits from criminals, politicians, bootleggers, communists. Our great Democratic President has kindled a revolutionary fire here in California that has us all by the throat. No food to be had. Everything at a standstill. Armed criminals riding the streets committing all manner of crimes. I am going now to join the police force here in Berkeley. I may pass on by it but I hope to get at least one enemy of society before I go. It's a continuous fight to keep on living.

Keep your boys back there on the E. S.

Your brother,

Thos N. Badger

John "Tank" Tankard Badger and Maggie Hallett Badger

John Badger, left, served as an army officer in Europe during World War II after graduating from Virginia Tech. Lamar served as an officer in the Army Corps of Engineers in the South Pacific.

The Depression Hits California

May 6, 1935

Dear Brother,

Your letter received. Am sorry to learn that you are in as bad a way financially as I am. If the banks close down on you, suppose they will take all you have. I have never been able to impart to you any of my ideas about management of property at home there. If you would let 3,000 hens or ducks produce your fertilizer free of charge, it would stop a big leak. The fertilizer men get all the potato money in the long run. I have only hell behind me and nothing else ahead of me. Have managed to pay interest and taxes and live on 5 cent meals up to now but I am in a jam. One tenant that pays $25 a month has quit. His wife is dying with a cancer. Doubt if he ever pays any more. All the others keep me guessing. I have no occupation now that the depression is on and I am barred by age from a job of any kind. The only satisfaction I can vision is 10 acres of production land. I will have to live on it alone.

My wife absolutely refuses to leave here. She is interested in her garden and likes to work all day in it. She has never had to bother with my finances – being a pauper here in town is terrific. My place down in the Santa Cruz Mts. would do but I am surrounded with bootleggers. Big still near me, 1,000 gallons a day. They know I am not one of them. The last day I spent there I thought more than once would be my last anywhere. Bullets were flying all day long. Federal, State and Co. officers are all in on it. Crime is running this country. Here we have all the races of people and I feel like a foreigner among them.

I intend to get 5 to 10 acres valley land to make a last stand. Have some wonderful figs I want to grow and a lot of other things including peanuts, Indian Summer Ducks, all kind of fruits and nuts. Our little fig here produced last year 200 lbs. You can live on figs and nuts and eggs and chickens and milk. Here money is our only food and I cannot stay here until I am completely broke. My health is wonderful. I make 20 miles over the mountains and climb 4,000 feet on Sunday and once or twice during the week. Come out some time and try to keep up with me.

Your brother,

Thos N. Badger

BOOTLEGGERS TAKING OVER

August 6, 1935

Dear Brother,

Your letter received. John is doing fine but nothing to what intensive poultry offers. All the money you have ever made came from animal husbandry – I would like to know the total amount guano (fertilizer) has taken from you? And you know potatoes are raised commercially in every state in the U.S. Intensive poultry fits in fine with your climate and soil. The U. S. Dept. of Ag recommends Northampton as ideal for poultry. Why not have your boy start in on a business of his own, his success depending on his own ability and industry and with the sky the limit of what can be done. Jobs have a way of leaving you. I have had no job since 1914, and the way things are going now I will be utterly poverty stricken in a short time. My wife refuses to go to the country. I expect to have to go alone or die in the poor house.

Your brother,

Thos N. Badger

TRAGEDY, PATHOS, AND HEARTACHE

February 9, 1936

Dear Brother,

Just a line or two to tell you how dark it is ahead of me. I am solely dependent on rents to live and they are failing me. Rents about half what they should be and I am unable to collect, as near as I can see I will be penniless in a very short time now. My wife is strong but her nerves are shattered. She may become helpless again now at any time and I have no money. I took her for a *walk in the hills yesterday. An automobile approached us and she became so excited that I had to hold her back to keep her from running in front of it. The tragedy, pathos and heartache of it all. I have planned to get a few acres of land to dig out a living on; but I am tied hand and feet and have been for a life time. I have managed to earn something up to about four years back. This last week used me up, nothing to do day after day year after year. 18,000 engineers in this state and most of them on relief. I believe I could make good in the country but if I put off going I will have nothing left to go with.*

Your brother,

Thos N. Badger

THE MATHMATICS OF RAISING POULTRY

March 7, 1937

Dear Brother,

Your letter received. I answered with a postal but I am going to call your attention to a subject I have presented to you before – What is your yearly guano bill? How many tons? Price? Lots of farmers here grow their own guano with poultry. They keep from 1,000 hens up to 5,000. Droppings from one hen will be 80 lbs per year. 5,000 hens produce 200 tons of dropping per year. They are best preserved by broadcasting and plowing under every 10 days as gathered otherwise nitrogen escapes in the air and other changes. Hens require per year 70 lbs grain or 175 tons for 5,000.

John intimated to me he wanted to start such a poultry plant. Why not set aside 10 acres for him to work on. This thing can be handled by one man if properly equipped. It is a certainty and good for a profit of $5,000 a year plus 200 tons guano, for which you pay around $40 a ton for chemicals not as good. John should hold on to his $1,800 a year job until he establishes himself. Teaching is a life job of unremuneration. I know a lot of U.C. professors who have spent their lives and are empty handed just as I am. He will need ten milk cows to help feed the poultry. Milk is indispensable in poultry. I expect to beat it back to the country yet myself. I hope I may.

Tom

My Heart Is On A Sitdown Strike

Sept. 15, 1937

Dear Brother,

Your letter received - $500 to you, $1,600 to fertilizer man. If you could rent ten acres to John for $1,600 you would cut out that $1,600 bill and do better than discount it 100%. What does John say? I have not made $1 for some 5 years now, and my time here is about up. The whole atmosphere is laden with choking oil and gas fumes, and they are killing people by thousands.

I would go down to my 40 acres and stay. I suppose more than likely I would be shot. I have lived so far on rents. Have collected gross $65,000. The place where I live can be rented for $75 a month and taxes are $12 a month.

My heart is on a sit down strike. My wife has a place in Petaluma and am going up there tomorrow to look it over. May move up there. We are both so near finished that we have not even the strength to make the move.

Thos. N. Badger

Planting Persimmons

January 11, 1938

Dear Brother,

Your letter received. Am sorry your late crops failed. Everything I know how to do has failed me, just now I have all of my places rented at a fair rental. Income I have been living on now for six long years. Every line of activity is stagnated. I am planting persimmon at Petaluma. The Huyu is the latest and finest and does well in Virginia. You would have to get the plant in September to avoid cold in transport. John can tell you about it. Root three scuppernongs for me next summer. I am planting 10 different kinds of grapes. You should try out the Pierce Grape, an Isabella seedling.

Tell John to get 100 White Indian Runner Ducks. They have one in Australia that laid 369 eggs in 1 year. They require no house. They eat a lot.

Your brother,

Thos. N. Badger

HOMESTEAD LAW

April 24, 1938

Dear Brother,

Your letter received. Homestead declaration is of no value if the property is mortgaged for all it will sell for. To be of any help, property must be free of encumbrances. My creditors may take all I have but cannot take my homestead, at least $5,000 is free if it is sold – Bankrupt Law is a Federal Law. I am certain you will find a provision in Virginia Law for homestead. If all your property is pledged for all you can borrow you had just as well forget about it.

The old home (Red Bank Landing) *is a natural Duck Ranch. The tides would not drown the ducks. White Indian Runners are small – 4 to 5 lbs. – and eat about same food as Leghorn chickens. 75lbs per year of grain and 75 lbs green stuff. The eggs are 1/3 larger than hen eggs and beautiful white. Suppose John tries out 100 and see what he can do. They do not require a house of any kind. Best have a roof over them and a cement floor which should be covered with sand and cleaned every day and they should have unpolluted water to drink and bathe in. They sell in New York at a premium. I intend to get a piece of Mother Earth somewhere if possible. Have been fortunate to hold on so far and have my wants satisfied. What will you do after Roosevelt forces you to pay $2.50 per day for labor? It may even be $5.00.*

Your brother,

Thos. N. Badger

What do the boys do with their earnings?

Hallet & Anna Badger Wedding Photos

BIG EVENT OF A LIFETIME

My mother and father, Anna Vaughan Badger and Thomas Hallett Badger, got married in the spring of 1938. Uncle Tom wrote them on June 2 to wish them "bon voyage" on the big event of a lifetime.

Dear Hallett,

Yours received. I wish you "bon voyage." It is the big event of a lifetime. Everything hinges on a happy marriage. There have been so many failures. Get in business for yourself as soon as possible, join the Masons, keep all of the commandments all of the time. Get physical exercise out in the open every day for at least two hours.

This country has been betrayed by Roosevelt and his gang. They are trying to start a revolution. Business is dead. It has taken all my thoughts and all my efforts to produce food for the past 10 years now. I have lived my life. I am 70 and packed to go.

Your uncle,

Thos. N. Badger

Roosevelt Put The U.S. on the Bum

September 12, 1938

Dear Brother,

Your letter came. Roosevelt has put the whole U.S. on the bum. Fruit here covers the ground, no market, and $4.00 a day for 8 hours for help. I am tied to the past as I have been for the past 15 years. I owe some $4,500. How much of a mortgage have you on the old place and what do you want for it?

Anyone living on Fowl Land (Fowling) Point? What could it be bought for? I am suffering now for want of occupation more than anything else. I might come back and try out the ducks. White Indian Runners appeal to me as a way to make a living. Ducks require <u>clean</u> salt water. Around all the big cities the water is full of filth. This bay here is loaded with it.

We will be past and gone now in a very short time so I do not worry. I go up in the hills for a half day twice a week. They are 2,000 feet to 4,000 feet on top of Mt. Diablo and I bring back some of the peace of Nature. My wife has been going for five mile trips with me for some time now.

Your brother,

Thos. N. Badger

Noisy Neighbors

May 28, 1943

Dear Brother,

Just a line. I am old and worn out, with no hope ahead. I have nothing to do to pass the time. On top of all this a dissolute woman has rented the house next to me and carries on 'til 4 o'clock in the morning night after night. I am getting desperate. I do not know what to do. I have been very sick lately from an absessed tooth but am coming back to life slowly since having it pulled. I feel this will eventually be my finish. Four years of this is beyond my ability to go through. We live on bread and water now. If I get strong enough to work, I shall try hard to go to work again. Your brother,

Thos. N. Badger

Notes to His Nephew

Tom wrote several notes to his nephew, Curtis Lamar Badger, the youngest son of Tank and Maggie. At this time, Lamar was serving in the U.S. Army Corps of Engineers during World War II, stationed in the South Pacific. Lamar didn't discuss his experiences in the war, but he entered the army as a private and was discharged at the end of the war as a major.

Post card from: Thomas N. Badger, Berkeley, California

TO: Lamar Badger

November 24, 1944

Dear Lamar,

Your letter reached me, and I am glad to hear from you again. Henry is down near you somewhere. If you like construction, why not keep right on with it? No use working for someone else, start building small houses if you can design and build so much the better. I have a lot of plans and instruments that I do not expect to use again. Will be glad to help you get going. I am nearly 80 year old and cannot remain here much longer.

Old again is tiresome indeed for an action man. I built hundreds of garages. $5 a month until paid for. Interest was 8%. I had some $10,000 out in them at one time and every last one was paid up.

Your uncle,

Thomas N. Badger

To: Mr. Curtis Lamar Badger

Birdsnest, Northampton Co., Virginia

November 11, 1947

Dear Lamar,

Yours received. Glad to hear from you again. We get only a living out of work for someone else. If we aspire for more we must start something. I travelled all along the road you are traveling now. If I had failed to venture outside I would be in the alms house. I may be anyway. Roosevelt left the country in the hands of communists. He sold us out for a contribution of votes - labor unions, Negroes and communists. He planned to be dictator, Franklin 1st. They are taking some $300 a month from me on rents and what is left does not cover expenses, paying mechanics $5 an hour $40 a day.

I will be 80 on December 2, 1947 and I know I will be here only a little longer. I hope what I have will see me through.

We are on the verge of civil war, at least everything points that way. The above is the plan of Russia to confiscate all private owner ship of land. My father had the Jungle Fever at Panama. He recovered except his nerves were out of control. He had the typhoid and nearly died. Outdoor physical work builds you up and enables you to recover.

Give my regards to all there at home.

Your uncle,

Thos N Badger

Letters from Dana Street

In the early 1950s Tom's return address changed from 2946 Linden Avenue in Berkely to 2504 Dana Street. Dana Street was the address of the Dana Sanitarium and Hospital, a nursing home that provided 24-hour service. Tom turned 83 in 1950, and his health began to deteriorate.

Tom continued to send letters to family back home, and when he became unable to write, he had a brother in his Masonic lodge do it for him. His brother Tank died in early 1953, and subsequent letters were sent to my father, Hallett.

From Jas. A. Wilson

Oakland, Calif.

January 7, 1953

Mr. Hallett Badger

Dear Sir,

I am writing this for your uncle, Tom Badger. I was out to see him today and delivered your last two letters, and also I phoned the telegraph office and had them read me your telegram, which I delivered to your uncle, and as you may know, he was very broken up over the news (of Tank's death).

He wished me to tell you it is very hard for him to write, as he is not feeling too well, but will try to get a letter off to you in a few days.

If there is anything you would like me to do or say for you, kindly let me know and I will be only too glad to attend to it.

Sincerely yours,

Jas. A. Wilson

Oakland, Calif.

March 8, 1953

Mr. T. Hallett Badger

I am very sorry of this delay in answering your last letter to your Uncle Tom. I went out to see him the day I received it and found him up and much better, but he seemed to be quite discouraged. He says as to the doctors he is suffering from creeping paralysis and is afraid to venture out for walks alone anymore. I promised to go out in a few days and go with him, but I came down with a kidney infection and have been in the hospital for the last week, but will go out as soon as I am able.

Your uncle wanted to be remembered to everyone and would like to write but is just not able. Hoping this finds you all okay.

I remain,

Jas. A. Wilson

Oakland, Calif.

April 6, 1953

Mr. Hallett Badger,

I hope you will excuse my delay in answering your last letter, but it seems I just could not get around to it.

I have been out to see your Uncle Tom a couple of times and have found him just about his regular self, he says he is getting a little weaker all the time, but I find him about the same. I took him out to do a little shopping. The place where he is staying is a rest home, and I would say it is about the average run of such places. His room is clean, but I do not know how the meals are. Your uncle says just about enough to keep him alive, but do not let *that worry you as you know how old people are. All in all, I think he is very well taken care of.*

I do not think there is anything you could do to help him at the present time. Hope this is the information you wanted. I am feeling quite myself again.

Would suggest you write to your uncle as often as you can as I know he enjoys hearing from you.

Sincerely yours,

Jas. A. Wilson

Uncle Tom died on January 24, 1954 at age 86. Services were held at the Telegraph Avenue Chapel of the Grant Miller Mortuaries, 2850 Telegraph Avenue, Oakland under the auspices of Oakland Lodge No. 188. He was cremated and his ashes were placed in the grave of his wife, Emily. The grave is in Mountain View Cemetery, 5000 Piedmont Avenue, Oakland, Plot 68, Grave 898. This obituary was published in the January 26, 1954 issue of the Berkeley Gazette:

Final rites were held today for Thomas Norman Badger, Berkeley resident for approximately 60 years, who died in a local rest home Sunday after a short illness. He was 84.

Born in Birdsnest, Va., Mr. Badger was the oldest living alumnae of Virginia Military Institute at the time of his death. A self-employed civil engineer and surveyor, Mr. Badger formerly lived here on Linden Ave. He retired nearly 10 years ago.

He was a member of Oakland Lodge No. 188 F and AM, and had been a member of the Sierra Club. Mr. Badger was active in local hiking organizations.

There are no immediate surviving relatives.

Services were held at Grant Miller Mortuary, 2850 Telegraph Ave., Oanland, with Oakland Lode No. 188, F and AM officiating. Committal was private.

And Now a Third Generation
of Thomas Badgers ...

Thomas Hallett Badger, II, whose great-great-uncle was Thomas N. Badger, lives in Oregon and made a trip to the San Francisco area in 2023 to explore the old family grounds. Here is his report on his visit:

Representing the third Thomas Badger to relocate from the Eastern Shore of Virginia to the west coast of the United States, I felt a pull to better understand the lives of my early relatives who took a similar journey. In April 2023, I traveled to the San Francisco area from my home in Oregon to retrace some of their steps and to find their final resting places. In doing so, I discovered more about their lives and found that Thomas W.'s travel and adventure continued even after his death.

Thomas Wyatt Badger - my great-great-great uncle. Died Nov 21, 1899.

Thomas W. Badger was originally buried at Laurel Hill Cemetery, located in present day downtown San Francisco, just south of the Presidio. During the second half of the nineteenth century, Laurel Hill Cemetery was the burial site of choice for influential citizens of the San Francisco area. Civic and military leaders, inventors, artists, and eleven United States Senators were buried at Laurel Hill.

When it opened in 1854, Laurel Hill was set on beautiful, sloping hills on the outskirts of San Francisco. As the city rapidly grew over the next five decades, it surrounded the cemetery. Around the turn of the century, local politicians targeted the cemetery for a housing development. The San Francisco Board of Supervisors closed the cemetery to more burials in 1902. Without revenue from new burials, the cemetery quickly fell into disrepair from lack of maintenance and vandalism. The Great San Francisco Earthquake in 1906 damaged many of the gravestones and other stoneworks. After a protracted legal battle, the cemetery was eventually closed in the 1930s. The Bay Area pioneers entombed at Laurel Hill were disinterred and their remains were moved into a mass grave at Cypress Lawn Memorial Park in Colma, CA over the course of several years.

Laurel Hill Cemetery was well known for its elaborate mausoleums and gravemarkers. When the cemetery was closed in the 1930s, families of those buried there were given the option to preserve gravemarkers, at their own cost. Due to economic factors of the Great Depression, most gravestones were abandoned. The City reclaimed the abandoned stones and repurposed them in breakwater projects along the Upper Great Highway on the western coastline of San Francisco. To this day,

The Laurel Hill Memorial commemorates the California Pioneers, the Forty-niners who settled in California prior to 1850 as the Gold Rush began. The last paragraph on the plaque reads as follows: "As you stand here open your heart to the Pioneers. They gave you great cities, a fair free land of mountains, a broad sea and the bluest of skies. Open your heart to them and trust the best that was in them all, and they will also give you wisdom and humor, and above all, courage. For they are your fathers."

This bronze sculpture depicts a California pioneer family in front of a semicircular concrete wall adorned with bronze and marble reliefs of an eagle, a schooner, and a covered wagon symbolizing westward movement. Plaque reads: THEIR VISIONS AND THEIR DREAMS CAME TRUE

gravestones appear in the dunes along the beach there after large storms. The stone model of the ship *Jane A. Falkenburg*, which marked the grave of Thomas W. Badger, likely now resides in those dunes.

According to the cemetery records, Thomas W. Badger's remains were moved to Cypress Lawn Memorial Park, to the WS-Laurel Hill plot, also known as The Laurel Hill Pioneer Mound, with the remains of approximately 35,000 other people from Laurel Hill Cemetery. Curiously, no records indicate the location of the remains of his wife, Jane Falkenburg Badger, or Charles Falkenburg, who were originally all buried alongside each other in Laurel Hill Cemetery.

While the Laurel Hill Pioneer Mound lacks any individual grave markers, the mound is marked with a large obelisk commemorating those earlier pioneers interred under the mound. In addition to the obelisk, there is large bronze and stone sculpture commemorating the pioneers, including the story of the how the remains found their final resting place at Cypress Hill Cemetery.

Thomas Norman Badger - my great, great uncle, son of John Wesley Badger, nephew of Thomas Wyatt Badger. Died January 24, 1954.

Thomas N. Badger was buried in Oakland, CA at Mountain View Cemetery, alongside his wife Emily Burns Badger. The cemetery has beautiful views of San Francisco Bay, the city, and the Golden Gate Bridge on a clear day. Thomas N.'s grave does not face these views, however. Thomas N.'s final resting spot directly faces the mountains above Berkeley that he climbed for years, including his own Badger Mountain, now named Grizzly Peak.

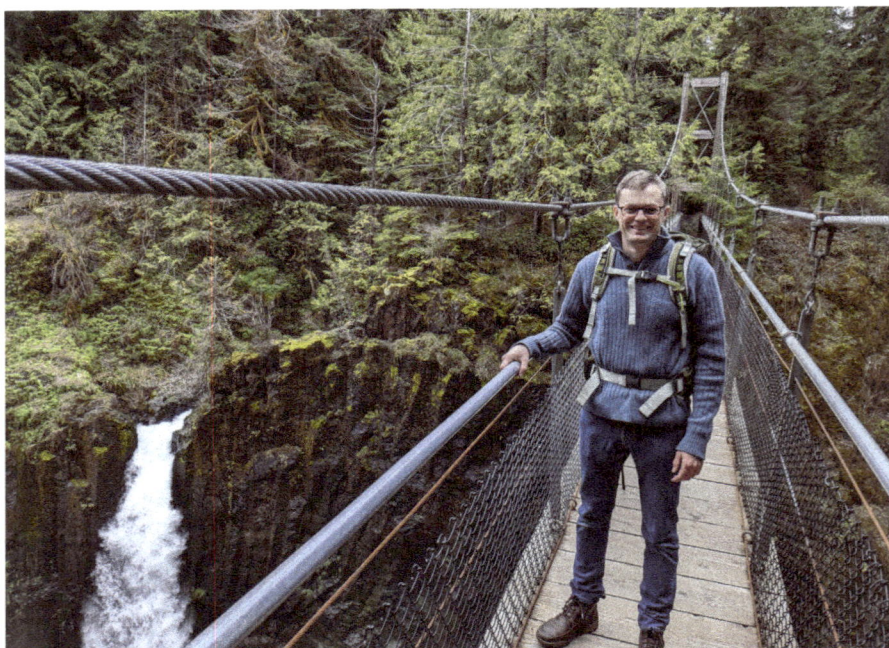

Tom Badger, like his great, great uncle, who was a founding member of the Sierra Club, is an avid hiker and a member of the Society of California Pioneers. Although he does not live in California, September 9, 1850 is a special day for him. It is Admission Day for the new state of California, a time for thoughtful celebration of all the fathers who came before and gave the best that was in them to create this fair free land.

APPENDICES

The following is a transcript of Capt. Badger's account of the *Central America* disaster. This account appeared in the *New York Journal of Commerce*, 21 September 1857, p. 2.

We left Havana on Tuesday, 8ᵗʰ September, in company with steamship Empire City. Made good weather until 10ᵗʰ. On the evening of the 10ᵗʰ there was every appearance of a gale or hurricane, ship still going on course and carrying full head of steam. The storm increased during the night and until Friday morning at 10 o'clock, the ship still making fine weather and keeping on her course. At 1 ½ o'clock on Friday afternoon the engine stopped, and on inquiring of the engineer, he said it was caused by the coal passers not passing the coal into the fire room with sufficient rapidity to keep the steam up. The waiters and stewards were then called upon and sent down to assist in passing coal. When the engine stopped, the ship fell off in the trough of the sea, and was at the mercy of the waves. The pumps worked by the engine, and which were the main dependence for keeping the vessel free of water, were also rendered useless.

The engine never made but one or two revolutions after this. I called the attention of the engineer to the fact that the water was gaining, the rolling of the ship forcing it in through the lee shaft hole, and proposed and did organize a gang for bailing. The deck pumps proving on trial to be out of order; bailing was the only recourse.

By this time the water had risen high enough to extinguish the lee fires, and the men employed in the coal hole and engine room were driven out by the steam and hot water. There was no longer any hope of again getting the machinery in operation. The principal leak was found to be around the lee shaft and at the lower dead lights. The ship was still staunch and sound, and not leaking at the bottom at all, and would have been in no danger if her machinery and pumps had been kept going.

At three o'clock on Friday afternoon I assisted in organizing and putting to work bailing gangs, to bail out, if possible, the engine-room and steerage.

The passengers joined willingly and cheerfully in this effort. An attempt was made to raise steam on the donkey engine to pump the ship out, using berths and other wood-work of the ship for fuel, but the engine would not work, from what cause was not known. At five o'clock, after consulting with Capt. Herndon, I assisted in cutting away the foremast, which somewhat relieved the ship. The ship had laid perfectly easy whilst the machinery was in motion, but she was in the trough of the sea, making heavy lurches to leeward.

At 5 o'clock on Friday, we rigged a drag (a spar with an anchor lashed to it), and paid it out to windward, in the hope of bringing her to the wind, but this had little or no effect.

From 4 o'clock until 8 in the evening we kept the water at bay, every man working with spirit and vigor.

From 12 o'clock to 4 o'clock on Saturday morning the water gained fast on us, as the men were fatigued and worn out by incessant labor and exposure to the storm. At 4 o'clock the gale somewhat abated, but a heavy sea continued, the water then being nearly up to the second cabin floor.

At daylight on Saturday morning, however, all hands took hold again with renewed vigor to free the ship. The water was then again kept at bay for an hour or two more, during which signals of distress were set, and a vigilant look-out kept for sails. The ladies were even anxious to assist up in bailing, and cheered us up in our labors by their calmness in these trying times. At 8 o'clock another attempt was made to raise steam in the donkey boiler so as to work the steam pumps, but the attempt failed, and all hope of relief from that quarter was abandoned.

At 10 o'clock on Saturday morning, the men again yielded to the severity of their labor, and the water again commenced to gain on us, but the bailing was still continued. At half past 1 o'clock a sail hove in sight, to the windward, which proved to be the Marine, of Boston. At 3 o'clock she rounded to at leeward of ship, when boats were lowered, bailing still going on. In lowering the boats two were stove by the heavy sea that still prevailed, which left only three, and one of them in a bad condition. By 5 o'clock we succeeded in putting on board the Marine all the women and children, twenty-six in number; during which the male passengers mostly continued at their work. The boats could not carry more than five or six, owing to the high sea, and they made several trips to and from the Marine. When the boat that took the last two ladies came alongside, the chief engineer jumped in the boat, and was followed by several other gentlemen. Two other boats came alongside afterwards, when there was a rush to jump in them by the male passengers, involving great danger. By this time the brig had drifted a long way to leeward, which made the trips of the boats long, and by this time it was dark, so that the boats did not again return.

About dark, a vessel, believed to be the schooner Sovereign, of New York, ran down under our lee. We hailed and told him that we were in sinking condition, asking him to lay by us all night, which he promised to do. The bailing in the meantime continued to progress, but the water had by this time raised halfway up the lower cabin, and was rapidly gaining on us. There was however, no cessation of the bailing until one hour before the ship sank, when all hope of keeping her afloat until daylight was relinquished. This was about seven o'clock on Saturday evening.

I should, however, mention that two hours previous I had a conversation with Captain Herndon, who after consultation agreed with me that the ship must go down, but it was still advisable to keep it up as long as possible, and we did not make known the result of our conversation, but urged all hands to renewed effort. Captain Herndon requested that second officer, Mr. Frazer, and myself should remain with him, and expressed his determination not to leave the ship while there was a soul on board, but would remain until she sunk from under him. His only regret was his family—and he died a brave man.

At 7 o'clock on Saturday night, the water was up to the floor of the dining saloon, and all then went to work calmly to devise means, each for their own safety. A half hour previous to the ship sinking there were two lights seen some distance to the leeward, supposed to be the brig Marine and the schooner that spoke to us an hour or two previous, but having a fresh breeze and high sea there were unable to work up to the windward.

A quarter of an hour before the steamer sank one of our boats hailed us, and a voice cried that his boat was stove and he could not take anyone on board. This boat was endeavoring to return from the Marine, but was disabled. It was doubtless the impression on board the brig and the schooner that the steamer would be able to keep up until morning, hence they probably did not keep as near during the night as they might have done. Indeed it was the opinion of many on board that we would hold up all night, and I did not think that she would go down before midnight.

At 10 minutes of 8 o'clock Captain Herndon took position on the wheel-houses with his second officer and fired rockets downward, the usual signal, to the brig and schooner that we were sinking rapidly. This was a fearful moment, and must have been also to the ladies on board the Marine, who understood the signal, all of whom had husbands or friends on board.

I now procured a board six feet long and six inches wide, tearing it off the front of a berth, and took my position on the taffrail, and held on the after awning stauncheon. At that time there were two or three hundred on the quarter deck, breathlessly awaiting the final sinking. There was two seas swept over the deck about this time, the last one sweeping nearly all the passenger on the main deck into the sea. The ship immediately after, at 8 o'clock on Saturday evening, sank, going down at an angle of 45 degrees, stern foremost. The suction of the ship drew the passengers under water for some distance, and threw them in a mass together. When they reached the surface the struggle for life was intense, with cries and shrieks for help, especially from those unable to swim. Many unable to swim clung to those who could, or laid hold of the larger pieces of the wreck, which were soon swamped. In ten minutes not less probably than three hundred had sunk to rise no more, whilst myself and others who had succeeded in holding on to some means of support were scattered over the dark and dreary ocean, floating off with the tide. There was a large number of the passengers had bags of gold dust, and some doubtless perished in their efforts to save it. I may also here add that from fifty to sixty passengers shut themselves up in the staterooms in despair, and sunk with the ship.

Those who had succeeded in keeping themselves afloat, soon scattered over the surface of the ocean for a distance of about a mile. One hour after the ship sank I saw a light at the leeward, which was seen by most of those rescued, supposed to be that of the schooner, *Sovereign*, but it soon disappeared. We knew that the ships to leeward could not reach us, and turned our gaze in the opposite direction.

At 1 o'clock on Sunday morning we saw approaching us, under full sail, with a strong breeze, the Norwegian bark, *Ellen*; ran into our midst, and those on watch were astounded with the cry of human beings. Captain Johnson, the commander, immediately hove his vessel to, under short sail, and commenced to rescue us. The steamer at this time had been down over five hours. He launched his boat, and threw out ropes and buoys, and done everything that good seamanship and a human heart could dictate to save as many as possible. I was the fourth one rescued, and witnessed the noble exertions of himself and crew throughout the night. He continued his search among the drift wood, tacking backward and forward, up to 12 o'clock on Sunday, but did not find anyone after 9 o'clock in the morning, and consequently relinquished the search at noon.

On the morning of Sunday the brig *Marine* was out of sight, and the schooner was some six miles to leeward, and appeared to be laying to, but soon bore away on her course, doubtless being satisfied that it was impossible to reach us, also seeing the bark backing and filling to windward.

The same day, at two o'clock, we spoke the bark *Saxony*, bound to Savannah; she reported seeing the brig with a number of ladies on board (supposed to be the *Marine*) under full sail steering north.

We bore away with a fair wind for Norfolk as the nearest port, and arrived off Cape Henry on Thursday evening, five of us reaching Norfolk in a pilot boat at daylight on Friday morning, which we had chartered for that purpose.

116

APPENDIX B

The Treasure of the *Central America*

When the *Central America* sank in September 1857 it took with it more than a ton of freshly minted gold coins and heavy gold bars worth probably a billion dollars in today's currency. The ship sank in water that was a mile-and-a-half deep, and although it was well known where the *Central America* went down, the treasure was for more than a century considered inaccessible.

That changed in 1987 when a group of young geologists and oceanographers from Columbus, Ohio convinced 120 investors that they had developed the technology to locate the treasure and recover it. Using a remote submarine called the *Nemo*, the group found the remains of the *Central America* off the coast of South Carolina. They filmed hundreds of uncirculated gold coins scattered across the bottom, and dozens of gold bars, some weighing more than 60 pounds. At such depths there was little sedimentation, and the current was gentle. Although the treasure had been on the bottom for 130 years, the photographs looked as though the coins had been casually placed across rotting timbers.

The group brought its first catch to Waterside in Norfolk in October 1989 and showed its collection of coins and gold bars to the public in a celebration widely covered by the press. Over the next three years, the Columbus-America Discovery Group used robots and computers to recover around a ton of gold, including many freshly minted, uncirculated gold coins that would be of incredible value to collectors. The discovery sparked years of legal wrangling involving the discovery team, investors, families of survivors, and numerous insurance companies that had paid claims 130 years ago.

The founder of Columbus-America, Tommy Thompson, was arrested by U.S. Marshalls in 2015. Thompson was accused of taking millions in gold bars and coins he helped recover. He has been in federal prison since then.

Crowds gathered at Waterside in Norfolk in 1989 to see the gold from the Central America.

APPENDIX C

Captain Badger Nears Death

The San Francisco Chronicle
November 2, 1899

Long Life of Captain Badger Ebbing Away
Rewarded Years Ago for Bravery

Captain Thomas W. Badger is seriously ill at his home in East Oakland, and but little hope is entertained for his recovery. The captain is one of the best known pioneers of the city, and indeed at one time owned a large portion of the territory on which Oakland is built. He is an old sailor-pioneer, having followed a life at sea until he landed in San Francisco on the 5th of August, 1849. For a long while he engaged in the shipping business in San Francisco, and had vessels trading all over the coast until 1872, when he retired from that business and interested himself in his public park at Brooklyn, East Oakland, which he purchased in 1861. Eleven years later he commenced building his great pavilion at Badger's Park, and after an expenditure of $50,000 Badger's Grand Central Park was thrown open to the public. The result was an immediate success, and his park, dancing hall, ten-pin alley, museum, amphitheater, menagerie, flower garden and sailing pond were very extensively patronized until they were destroyed by fire many years ago.

One of the most valued possessions of the old captain was presented to him in 1858. It was a silver trumpet, subscribed for by citizens "in token of their high appreciation of Captain Badger's conduct on board the steamer Central America at the time of the loss of that ill-fated vessel." The steamer was on a trip from Aspinwall to New York and in rough weather was wrecked. Her captain and officers were among the lost and Captain Badger assumed management of the foundering steamer, which he kept afloat until relief came from a Norwegian bark. To his efforts was attributed the saving of nearly 200 lives. On arriving in New York the citizens at once subscribed to give him a memento of their recognition of his bravery, and he could just as easily have

119

had a large sum of money as a silver trumpet, but he declined, although in the wreck he lost $20,000 in coin which he had made in California.

Under the administration of Governor Haight Captain Badger was a Pilot Commissioner of San Francisco, and held the office for many years. His large holdings have very materially decreased, and about two years when the City Council proposed to make some very extensive improvements near Badger's Park the old captain appeared before that body and said that if the Council were determined to carry out these improvements it would bankrupt him entirely. He closed a very earnest appeal by telling them that after he was gone would be time enough to go ahead with the proposed work.

• BADGER FUNERAL.

Last Rites Over the Old East Oaklander.

Friends of Pioneer Days Gathered to Pay the Last Respects to the Deed.

The funeral of Captain Thomas W. Badger was held from his late residence, 953 Seventh avenue, East Oakland, shortly before noon yesterday. Many of the old residents of the city were in attendance. The floral offerings were numerous, one most noteworthy being a large anchor, typical of the early life of the deceased.

Among those present at the funeral were Drs. Harry and William Bell of San Francisco, and Thomas W. Badger, nephews of the deceased.

The services were conducted by Rev. William C. Shaw, rector of the Church of the Advent, East Oakland, and by Rev. Hamilton Lee of Martinez, who was formerly rector of the Church of the Advent at a time when Captain Badger was a regular attendant there Appropriate musical selections were rendered by a quartette.

The pallbearers were C. H. King, O. I. Denison, Kirkham Wright, W. C. Mason, E. H. Shaw, and J. W. Dutton. The interment was at Laurel Hill cemetery, San Francisco.

Aunt Easter Badger, from the Badger-Tankard book

AUNT EASTER BADGER

by

Margaret Badger Dunton

A short story about a little slave girl, born about 1827. Aunt Easter was the daughter of a slave belonging to Thomas and Margaret Badger. As was the custom of the time, she was given the duty of guarding my father against all harm as he played around while he was a very small child. She was very proud of the fact that she was "brung" up in the house by the missus and not out with the slaves. She was the slave of John W. Badger from his birth until he went to California in 1849, when he gave her her freedom. At one time she was cook at "The Tavern" at Eastville. As soon as John Badger returned to the Eastern Shore and married, she cooked for him.

During the Civil War, when the Yankees took control of Northampton County, they took her two sons and put them in the Federal army. She never saw them nor heard from them again. She had one brother, Uncle Stepney Badger, who lived near our home. She was devoted to my father as long as he lived. After his death, she lived with his widow and children until she died in 1908.

Aunt Easter had many peculiar ideas and a dialect all her own. She believed in witchcraft. She though an enemy could put an evil spell on a person if they set a bottle for them. I remember she told me you had to put a hair from a horse's tail and a few other things in a bottle and put them under the steps, over which the person whom you wished to harm, had to pass. When the person passed over this bottle the evil spell possessed them.

She once told me that her old mistress wanted to teach her to read but she did not want to learn, which she later regretted very much.

When I was a child she often cooked her own food in the fireplace.

She often said "de cook stove is de most spensive thing dat ever come in dis county."

She loved my father very dearly and would do anything for him. I have heard her say "if Mars John ud die ide leave here fore de kittle ud git hot." She often said, "gin in time, you'l be in time."

About once a year she would go to see some of her friends and take all her clothes. I asked her why she was taking them all. She said, "I want em to know I got em." If the dogs, cats, and children were playing on the floor she would say they were "skiffling on the floor." Mars John liked to go to Marionville and Miss Sue liked to go to Franktown. Aunt Easter used to say "Marionville is Marse John's Heavenly Hole and Franktown is Miss Sue's Heavenly Hole."

Often people would send their love to her. She would say, "what did they send it in?" meaning a gift. They usually sent her something. When she spoke of potatoes, they were "taters"; tomatoes were "mottoses"; asparagus was "sparegres"; animals were "critters".

She always had a hot cup of coffee for Marse John when he got up in the morning. This was made in the fireplace and kept warm until he got up. I often ate some of the things she cooked for herself in the fireplace. I enjoyed them.

Sometimes I read to her. At night when her legs hurt her I used to rub them in hot vinegar. In her last days, Mama and I nursed her until she passed away in 1908. She loved me better than she loved anyone except Marse John and I loved her as I loved my own family.

"Aunt Easter" Badger died in the summer of 1908 and was buried in the colored burying ground. She was a member of Johnson's Methodist Church and sat in the balcony.

Appendix E

The Obituary of Mary Frances "Fannie" Badger

This obituary was clipped from a newspaper and the date and name of the newspaper were not on the clipping. From reading other stories on the clipping, the newspaper appeared to be a religious publication.

Obituary of Mrs. Fannie T. Badger

Died June 16, 1871

Died, June 16th, 1871, in the town of Fredericksburg, at the residence of Mr. James W. Ford, MRS. FANNIE T. BADGER, in the 31st year of her age.

Mrs. B. was the wife of J. W. Badger, and daughter of John and Susan Tankard, all of Northampton county, VA. Besides these, she leaves two small children and a large circle of friends to mourn her loss. She was the eldest daughter of pious parents, and having early been taught the principles of Christianity, embraced religion when quite young. At the age of fourteen she united herself with the M. E. Church (Methodist Episcopal), South, of which she continued a consistent member and firm supporter as long as she lived.

In the death of Mrs. B. the community and church have sustained an irreparable loss. A modest and sincere Christian, a devoted wife and mother, a kind and sympathetic friend, she ever exemplified the virtues and graces that adorn and beautify a womanly and Christian character.

Her death occurred under painful and trying circumstances – away from her home and family, where she had gone for the benefit of her health and to visit fond relatives. On the same day that she had proposed to return home, her spirit took its flight to another world and the very time she was to have arrived at the wharf, and had written her husband and friends to meet her, she was brought back a lifeless body – a corpse. Such is the uncertainty of life!

Although her last illness was brief, she had been in declining health for the last ten or eleven months, during which time she had been subject to severe paroxysm of pain, all of which she bore with uncomplaining fortitude and resignation. The writer has witnessed many cases of suffering, but none where a greater degree of heroic and patient forbearance was exhibited. This same cheerful Christian resignation accompanied her to the end. And when told that she must die, although much regretting that she could not see her husband and two little boys and give them her parting blessing, she was, nevertheless, willing to leave them in the care of "Him who doeth all things well," and sent each of them, as well as other relatives, the message to "meet her in heaven." After this she departed, rejoicing in the "hope of the glory of God."

She evidently manifested, by her willingness to die, especially during her last illness, that she had made death the subject of much previous thought and reflection. She acknowledged her unworthiness and shortcomings, but said the Saviour's grace is all sufficient — that in Him she had believed, in Him she had trusted, and with Him she soon expected to live — where there would be no more sickness or suffering.

May our end be like hers.

www.ingramcontent.com/pod-product-compliance
Lightning Source LLC
Chambersburg PA
CBHW040136270326
41927CB00019B/3400